TABLE OF CON

CM009085327

1. THAI PRAWN SALAD 3

2. CHOPPED THAI SALAD WITH SESAME GARLIC DRESSING 5

3. CRUNCHY THAI SALAD WITH PEANUT DRESSING 7

4. THAI RED CURRY NOODLE SOUP 9

5. REFRESHING CUCUMBER SOUP 10

6. COCONUT CHICKEN SOUP RECIPE 11

7. THAI CHICKEN NOODLE SOUP 12

8. TOM YUM KOONG SOUP 14

9. THAI PUMPKIN SOUP 15

10. THAI HOT-AND-SOUR SHRIMP SOUP (TOM YAM KUNG) 16

11. THAI PUMPKIN SEAFOOD STEW 18

12. CRISPY FLUFFY FISH W/ GREEN MANGO SALAD 21

13. TAMARIND PRAWN CURRY 24

14. THAI STEAMED MUSSELS 25

15. SARDINE AND LEMONGRASS SALAD 26

16. PEPPERY GARLIC SHRIMP 27

17. TILAPIA IN THAI SAUCE 28

18. THAI BANANA SALSA WITH KING PRAWNS 29

19. THAI-STYLE BEEF WITH BASIL AND CHILIES (PHAT BAI HORAPHA) ... 31

20. THAI PORK DUMPLINGS 33

21. PORK BELLY DRUNKEN NOODLES 35

22. THAI-STYLE GRILLED PORK SKEWERS (MOO PING) RECIPE 37

23. THAI WATERFALL BEEF SALAD - A FEAST OF FLAVOR! 39

24. BEEF SATAY WITH THAI PEANUT SAUCE 41

25. LAMB CUTLETS WITH THAI STYLE DRESSING 44

26. BEEF AND BROCCOLI – THAI STYLE 45

27. PORK & HOLY BASIL STIR-FRY 48

28. THAI BASIL MINCED PORK 49

29. GARLIC LOVERS THAI BASIL CHICKEN 50

30. THAI FRIED CHICKEN 52

31. CREAMY COCONUT LIME CHICKEN 55

32. THIS CLASSIC THAI CHICKEN FRIED RICE IS SIMPLE YET TASTY 56

33. CLASSIC SESAME NOODLES WITH CHICKEN 58

34. THAI CHICKEN BALLS 59

35. CHICKEN MASSAMAN CURRY 60

36.Thai Cashew Chicken Stir Fry 62

37.Pineapple Chicken Satay 64

38.Thai green prawn curry 66

39.Thai Monkfish Curry 67

40.Thai Yellow Chicken Curry With Potatoes 68

41.Paul Mercurio's pork and pumpkin red curry recipe 69

42.EASY COCONUT SHRIMP CURRY 71

43.Vegan Broccoli Chickpea Curry 73

44.Thai Green Curry..75

45.Curried Coconut Chicken...77

46.Sweet Thai Shrimp Curry with Peanut Noodles. 78

47.Panang curry 80

48.Stir-Fried Mushrooms with Baby Corn 82

49.Sesame Ginger Bok Choy 83

50.THE EASIEST VEGETABLE STIR FRY 84

51.Thai Morning Glory Stir Fry...85

52.Authentic Thai pumpkin stir fry recipe 86

53.Mango Rice Pudding 89

54.Fresh Fruit Bowl 90

55.Green Banana Fries 91

56.Green Papaya Salad 92

57.Ginger Soy Chicken over Jasmine Rice...93

58.Thai Rice Pudding 95

59.Thai Mango Sticky Rice Dessert...97

60.Easy Creamy Coconut Black Beans 99

62.Tom Yum Fried Rice..100

63.Thai Green Curry Fried Rice 102

64.Thai Pineapple Fried Rice 103

65.Restaurant Style Coconut Rice (Coconut Milk) 105

THE END 106

1. THAI PRAWN SALAD

Prep Time10 minutes

Cook Time10 minutes

Servings2 people

Calories439kcal

INGREDIENTS

Prawn Salad

- 600 grams/1.3 pounds whole medium green prawns
- ½ teaspoon Freshly ground white pepper
- 1 tablespoon Soy sauce
- 1 tablespoon Olive/Coconut oil
- 2 medium Shallots thinly sliced
- 1 cup Green beans cut into 3 cm lengths
- 2 cups Zucchini Noodles
- 1 cup Coriander/Cilantro leaves
- 1 cup Mint leaves
- 1 cup Thai basil leaves
- 1 baby gem lettuce leaves torn
- Zest of 1 Lime
- ½ cup dried shallots

Chilli and Lime Dressing

- ⅓ cup Fresh lime juice
- ¼ cup Fish sauce
- 1 long fresh red chilli deseeded and finely chopped
- 3 teaspoons Ginger very finely grated
- 4 tablespoons stevia or other natural sweetener that measures like sugar

INSTRUCTIONS

1. Peel the prawns and discard the heads before cooking. Depending on their size, peel and devein the prawns, then slice them into two or three large chunks.

2. Chilli and Lime Dressing: In a bowl, whisk together all of the dressing ingredients until smooth. You may also shake it in a jar with a tight-fitting cover. About two-thirds of a cup of dressing is needed.

3. Set aside 15 minutes before cooking to marinate the prawn flesh in fresh shallots, white pepper, soy sauce and 14 of the chilli lime dressing.

4. In a large pan or wok, heat the oil over medium-high heat. Add the prawns and cook, stirring occasionally, until they are pink and opaque. Add the prawns and heat for another 5 minutes, or until the marinade is crispy and the prawns are cooked through, depending on your preference. Set aside when you've removed it from the pan.

5. In a basin of boiling water, add zucchini noodles and beans until they are barely submerged, then drain and set aside. Drain them once they've sat for five minutes.

6. In a large bowl, combine zucchini noodles and beans. Chilli and lime dressing with 14 cup of dried shallots should be added, as well as the herbs, lettuce and lime zest. In a large bowl, add all of the ingredients and toss well. Toss in the prawns and toss some more. You may serve it right away with some more dressing and dried shallots.

2.CHOPPED THAI SALAD WITH SESAME GARLIC DRESSING

TOTAL TIME: 25 minutes

YIELD: 6 1x

INGREDIENTS

For the dressing:

- 1/3 cup canola oil
- 3 cloves garlic, peeled
- 3 tablespoons low sodium soy sauce
- 2 tablespoons water
- 2 tablespoons white distilled vinegar
- 2 tablespoons honey
- 1 tablespoon sesame oil
- 1 tablespoon lemongrass paste (ginger would also work)
- a squeeze of lime juice

For the salad:

- 16 ounces frozen shelled edamame
- 5–6 cups baby kale
- 3 large carrots
- 2 bell peppers (1 red, 1 yellow)
- 1 cup cilantro leaves
- 3 green onions
- 3/4 cup cashews (if you can find them, Trader Joe's Thai Lime and Chili Cashews are the bomb)

INSTRUCTIONS

1. In a food processor, combine all of the dressing ingredients until smooth. Make adjustments based on how you like it. Rinse the food processor and store the dressing in a container for later use.

2. To prepare the edamame, place it in a saucepan of boiling water and cook for 3 to 5 minutes. Drain and let it cool before serving. Cut up the kale, carrots, peppers and cilantro leaves into thin strips or shreds while you're waiting for the sauce to thicken.

3. Process 5 times in the food processor to create a minced texture from the edamame. Toss the cashews into a separate basin and repeat the process. Make sure the kale, carrots, peppers and cilantro are all mixed together before adding the green onions and cashews. Serve immediately after drizzling with the dressing and tossing lightly a few times.

3. CRUNCHY THAI SALAD WITH PEANUT DRESSING

Prep: 30 mins
Total Time: 30 mins
Yield: 4 servings

INGREDIENTS

Thai Salad

- 2 cups kale
- 1 ½ cups napa cabbage
- 1 ½ cups red cabbage
- ½ cup red bell pepper
- ½ cup carrot
- 1 mango
- ¼ cup cilantro
- 8 mint leaves
- 1 tablespoon green onions
- ¼ cup peanuts roasted, roughly chopped

Peanut Dressing

- ⅓ cup peanut butter natural creamy or smooth
- 2 tablespoons lime juice
- 3 tablespoons honey or pure maple syrup
- 1 ½ tablespoons rice wine vinegar
- 1 ½ tablespoons soy sauce low sodium
- 1 teaspoon sesame oil
- 1 teaspoon sriracha
- ½ teaspoon ginger minced
- 1 clove garlic roughly chopped
- 1 tablespoon water

INSTRUCTIONS

Thai Salad

1. Add the kale, cabbage, bell pepper, carrot, mango, cilantro, mint, and green onion to a large bowl and toss to combine. Make the dressing as you do this.

Peanut Dressing

1. It's time to get your hands on some PB&J! In a blender combine the following ingredients: peanut butter lime juice honey vinegar soy sauce sesame oil garlic and water
2. Puree for approximately a minute until smooth and blended. The ingredients can also be combined in a medium-sized bowl and stirred together.
3. If required, add extra water to thin down the dressing. Salt and pepper to taste, if necessary.

4. THAI RED CURRY NOODLE SOUP

INGREDIENTS

- 2 Tbsp. avocado oil or olive oil
- 1/2 cup diced yellow onion
- 1/2 cup diced red bell pepper
- 1/2 cup diced carrots
- 3 garlic cloves, minced
- 1 Tbsp. freshly grated ginger
- 1/4 cup red curry paste
- 6 cups chicken broth or vegetable stock
- 1 (14 oz.) can full-fat coconut milk
- 3 Tbsp. fish sauce
- 4–5 oz. ramen or rice noodles (see note)
- 1 Tbsp. fresh lime juice, plus more to taste
- 1/2 cup fresh chopped cilantro, plus more for serving
- Lime wedges, for serving

INSTRUCTIONS

1. A dutch oven may be used to heat the oil. Cook the vegetables before adding them to the dish. Cook for 5-7 minutes, or until the meat is cooked.
2. Add the garlic, ginger, and red curry paste to the mixture and mix thoroughly. Stirring constantly, cook for 1 minute or until aromatic.
3. Add fish sauce, chicken broth, and coconut milk. Salt and pepper to taste, if necessary. Simmer for a few minutes before removing from the heat. For 5 minutes, cook the dish uncovered. Add noodles and boil until they are

tender. Different types of noodles have different cooking times. Look at the instructions on the packaging.

4. Incorporate the lime juice and cilantro into the mixture and serve.

5.REFRESHING CUCUMBER SOUP

Prep: 20 mins

Additional: 1 hr

Total: 1 hr 20 mins

Yield: 8 servings

INGREDIENTS

- 4 cucumbers - peeled, seeded, and coarsely chopped
- 1 small garlic clove, chopped
- 3 cups chicken broth, divided
- 2 ½ cups sour cream
- 3 tablespoons white vinegar
- 2 tablespoons seasoned salt (such as LAWRY'S®)

Directions

1. In a blender, combine the cucumbers, garlic, and 1 cup of chicken broth. Blend in the remaining 2 cups of chicken stock, sour cream, vinegar, and seasoned salt until completely smooth. Soup should be refrigerated for at least an hour before serving.

6.COCONUT CHICKEN SOUP RECIPE

PREP TIME: 15 MINUTES

COOK TIME: 30 MINUTES

TOTAL TIME: 45 MINUTES

YIELD: 8

INGREDIENTS

- 1 tablespoon olive oil
- 1-inch piece peeled fresh ginger, thinly sliced*
- 1 tablespoon dried lemongrass
- 8 ounces mushrooms, stemmed and sliced
- 6 cups chicken stock or broth
- 3 tablespoons lime juice
- 1/2 teaspoon red pepper flakes
- 1 pound rotisserie/roasted chicken, shredded
- 1 3/4 cups unsweetened coconut milk (about 1 13.5-ounce can)
- 2 tablespoons Asian fish sauce**
- 3 tablespoons chopped fresh cilantro leaves

INSTRUCTIONS

1. Add the oil to a big pot and bring it to a boil. Stir in the ginger and lemon grass, toasting for approximately two minutes, until they're aromatic. After 2 minutes, add mushrooms and continue stirring.
2. Cook for 8-10 minutes with the stock, lime juice, and red pepper flakes added to the pot. Remove big bits of ginger if they are bothering you (an Asian spider will help do the job, of course a slotted spoon works too).
3. After approximately 4-5 minutes, add the chicken.

4. Slowly add the coconut milk, fish sauce, and cilantro; bring the heat down to medium and let the flavors meld for approximately 10 minutes. Salt and pepper to your liking..
5. Chilli oil, cilantro leaves, and lime wedges can be added to the dish as desired.

7.THAI CHICKEN NOODLE SOUP

Prep Time: 20 mins

Cook Time: 40 mins

Total Time: 1 hour

Yield: 4

INGREDIENTS

- 2 tablespoons coconut or olive oil
- 1 onion, finely diced (or 2 large shallots)
- 2 tablespoons ginger, peeled and finely chopped
- ¼ cup lemongrass, very finely chopped (or use 3 tablespoons paste)
- ¼ cup, thinly sliced galanga root (peels ok) (or use 3 tablespoons paste)
- 4 cloves garlic, chopped
- 8 cups chicken stock or chicken broth
- 2 cups water
- 1 teaspoon salt
- 6–8 lime leaves (check the frozen section of the Asian market, if not fresh)
- 1 ½ lbs chicken breast (or thigh) sliced into uniform ½ inch thick, bite-size pieces

- 4 oz sliced mushrooms (optional)
- 4–6 oz. vermicelli rice stick noodles, kelp noodles or angel hair pasta
- 2–3 teaspoons fish sauce, more to taste
- lime juice to taste (start with 1/2 a small lime)
- 2–3 teaspoons chili paste (optional)

Garnishes:

- ½ Cup chopped cilantro
- 4 scallions chopped
- 1 fresh red chili pepper- medium hot
- 1 lime cut into wedges
- bean sprouts (optional, but delish)
- hot chili sauce (sriracha, sambal or hot chili oil)

INSTRUCTIONS

1. The oil should be heated at medium-high heat in a big saucepan. Toss in onion and cook for 2-3 minutes on medium-low heat. Sauté for a few more minutes before adding ginger and lowering the temperature to medium-low. Add galanga, garlic, and lemongrass to the soup (optional). Stirring every 3 to 5 minutes until fragrant, roughly 3 to 5 minutes total. After that, include chicken stock, water, salt, and lime leaves. Bring the stock to a boil, then lower the heat to a simmer for around 10-15 minutes. Adding chillies to the boiling stock will make it overly hot, so don't do it.)
2. Noodles and mushrooms can be added at this point, and the stock should be kept at a low boil until the chicken is cooked through and the noodles are done, around 7 minutes.
3. Add a substantial amount of lime juice and fish sauce.

4. Salt, acidity and spice may all be adjusted using fish sauce, lime juice and chili paste to suit your taste. Stir in half of the scallions right before serving.
5. As soon as the soup is served, garnish the bowls with chopped cilantro, scallions and bean sprouts (optional, but they provide a nice crunch), as well as a few red slice chilies and a lime wedge.

8.TOM YUM KOONG SOUP

Prep: 10 mins

Cook: 40 mins

Additional: 20 mins

Total: 1 hr 10 mins

Yield: 4 -6 servings

INGREDIENTS

- ½ pound medium shrimp - peeled and deveined
- 12 mushrooms, halved
- 1 (4.5 ounce) can mushrooms, drained
- 4 cups water
- 2 lemon grass
- 4 kaffir lime leaves
- 4 slices galangal
- 4 chile padi (bird's eye chiles)
- 1 ½ tablespoons fish sauce
- 1 ½ limes, juiced
- 1 teaspoon white sugar
- 1 teaspoon hot chile paste
- 1 tablespoon tom yum soup paste (Optional)

DIRECTIONS

1. To make matchstick-sized pieces, trim the lemongrass.
2. After removing the shrimp heads and shells from the water, simmer for 20 minutes. Turn off the stove. Before discarding the heads and shells, soak them for a further 20 minutes.
3. To make matchstick-sized pieces, trim the lemongrass.
4. Salt, sugar and chili paste are added to a saucepan of water and brought to a boil before the stock is added. Add the shrimp and both mushrooms after 5 minutes of cooking. Cook another 10 minutes. Coriander leaves can be used as a garnish.

9.THAI PUMPKIN SOUP

Prep Time: 5 minutes

Cook Time: 8 minutes

Total Time: 13 minutes

Servings: 6 servings

INGREDIENTS

- 2 cans pumpkin puree 15 ounce cans
- 1 can coconut milk 13.5 ounce can, 2 tablespoons separated
- 4 cups chicken broth
- 2 tablespoons red curry paste
- 1/2 teaspoon cayenne pepper
- 1 red chili pepper sliced for garnish

INSTRUCTIONS

1. In a saucepan or soup pot, boil the curry paste until aromatic (about 1 minute), then add the pumpkin puree and chicken stock and simmer for about 5 minutes. Stir until all of the ingredients have been incorporated into a homogenous mixture.
2. For 3 minutes, stir occasionally, then add the coconut milk and cayenne pepper powder and cook for another 3 minutes. Add more water if necessary.
3. For a further 3 to 5 minutes (stirring regularly), bring the soup to a boil and then reduce the heat to low. Then serve the soup in individual servings.
4. Coconut milk and red chili pepper slices should be drizzled over the soup before serving. Serve immediately.

10. THAI HOT-AND-SOUR SHRIMP SOUP (TOM YAM KUNG)

INGREDIENTS

- 2 cups Thai Pork Broth or water
- 2 Tbs. Thai fish sauce, such as Tiparos or Squid
- 4 Thai or serrano chiles, preferably green, smashed gently; more to taste
- 6 thin 1-inch slices fresh lemongrass, lightly crushed
- 4 very thin slices fresh galangal or ginger
- 6 wild lime leaves, torn, or 1 Tbs. finely grated lime zest
- 1 Tbs. crushed cilantro root or chopped cilantro stem
- 1 tsp. granulated sugar; more to taste

- 5 oz. oyster mushrooms, torn into bite-size pieces (about 2 cups)
- 6 small shallots, preferably Asian red, peeled and halved
- 8 jumbo shrimp (21 to 25 per lb.; preferably wild), peeled and deveined
- 2 Tbs. fresh lime juice
- 1 Tbs. thinly sliced sawtooth coriander or cilantro
- 1 Tbs. thinly sliced scallions

INSTRUCTIONS

1. A 3- to 4-quart saucepan should be filled with broth or water, fish sauce, chiles, lemongrass, galangal, lime leaves, cilantro root, and sugar. Bring to a boil, then lower the heat and simmer for about 15 minutes.
2. Remove from heat when mushrooms and shallots are tender, 2 to 5.
3. Add the shrimp and the lime juice and mix it all together well. Sugar and chilies, to taste.) The soup should be spicy, sour, and salty. There should be no sweetness in the soup; the sugar is there to counterbalance the other tastes.) Cook for 2 to 3 minutes, or until the shrimp are barely pink.
4. Garnish with scallions and sawtooth coriander.

11.THAI PUMPKIN SEAFOOD STEW

Servings: 8

Prep: 30 mins

Cook: 15 mins

Total: 45 mins

INGREDIENTS

- 1 13.5-ounce can coconut milk
- 1 1/2 tbsp fresh galangal
- roughly chopped (substitution = 1 tbsp. ginger)
- 1 tbsp lemongrass
- minced
- 8 each kaffir lime leaves
- chopped (substitution = 1 tsp. lime zest)
- 4 each garlic cloves
- roughly chopped
- 1 small (2 to 3 lb.) kabocha squash (substitution = acorn
- buttercup, delicata, pumpkin)
- 32 medium-sized clams
- fresh and alive
- 32 medium-sized mussels
- fresh and alive
- 1 1/2 lb fresh salmon
- 1 lb shrimp
- 2 tbsp coconut oil
- 16 leaves thai basil
- hand torn (substitution = regular basil)
- salt and pepper
- to taste

INSTRUCTIONS

1. Add the coconut milk, galangal, lemongrass, lime leaves, and garlic to a small saucepan and bring it to a boil over medium heat. Bring to a simmer over low heat. Simmer for 30 minutes, then remove from heat and leave it "steep" in the pot. Stir, if necessary.

2. A constant spray of cold water from a faucet into a bowl of cold water is a great way to keep your fresh seafood fresh while the coconut milk steeps in the aromatics. This helps remove some of the salinity and sand from the water. Let the water drip on this for a while.

3. Make sure your pumpkin is ready to eat. First, I prefer to remove the outer layer, which is needless and time-consuming (I use a knife and cut it off, like a cantaloupe). It's up to you. After that, split it in half and use a spoon to remove the seeds from the inside. Then, slice it into pieces that are approximately half an inch to three-quarters of an inch wide. To ensure consistent cooking, they should be be the same size. Set away for a later time.

4. Using your hands, scoop up the clams and mussels from the bowl and move them to another. Keep the original bowl's sand and debris in place. Rinse and dry the original bowl, then put it away. We'll put it to good use once more. Slowly pour cold water over the next dish of clams and mussels.

5. Make sure to remove the large vein that runs down the back of your shrimp before cooking. It's entirely up to you whether or not to peel the clams and mussels; I did so because the shells were still in there.

6. Bite-sized chunks of fresh fish should be used. You may use whatever kind of fresh fish you choose (halibut, sole, snapper, etc.) as long as it's decent quality.

7. Once more, transfer your clams and mussels. Remove the mussels' beards using a damp cloth.
8. To do this, grasp the beard with the towel and clamp it tightly between your fingers before pushing OUT and toward the hinge. This should get the job done for most people, though others may find it easier. As a last step, if you find that your mussel shells have a lot of barnacles or detritus stuck to them, it may be a good idea to clean them. To dry your clams and mussels, remove them from the dish and set them on a dry cloth or in a colander.
9. Using a fine strainer, strain the coconut milk mixture into a large soup pot and cover it with a lid. The fibrous remnants should be thrown away. To begin, heat up your coconut milk combination. Slowly bring it to a boil.
10. A big sauté pan should be preheated at medium-high heat. Your oil should be poured into the pan and swung about. Add the kabocha to the pan and spread it out evenly on the bottom of the pan as soon as it begins to ripple. These tiny cubes need a little color to liven them up. Add a little salt and pepper to taste. For approximately 5 minutes, cook them until they begin to soften and develop a little color. Add them to the coconut milk mixture and stir them in.
11. To begin, heat a large sauté pan over medium-high heat. Your oil should be poured into the pan and swung about. Add the fish and shrimp to the pan as soon as the water ripples and season with salt and pepper. Make sure the bottom of the pan is equally covered in it. We'd want to give the fish a little color.
12. You may add the clams and mussels to the coconut milk mixture while the fish and shrimp are cooking.

13. Toss in the fish/shrimp and clams/mussels after about 2 minutes of sautéing, remove the lid, add the fish/shrimp to the coconut milk, and then return the top.
14. Simmer for another 4 to 5 minutes, or until the mixture is thick and creamy. Only around 12 minutes should elapse between the time you begin sautéing the kabocha and the time you consume. Everything goes swiftly once it's all set up and ready to go.
15. Add the fresh basil just before serving.

12. CRISPY FLUFFY FISH W/ GREEN MANGO SALAD

Yield: Serves 4

INGREDIENTS

Mango Salad

- Thai chilies, to taste
- 2 Tbsp finely chopped palm sugar
- 2 Tbsp fish sauce
- 2 Tbsp lime juice
- ½ shallot, thinly sliced
- 1 heaping Tbsp dried shrimp, chopped
- 1 sour green mango, julienned (see note)
- 2 Tbsp chopped cilantro

Fish

- 250 g fish meat of any kind
- A pinch of salt or 1 tsp soy sauce
- 3 Tbsp roasted peanuts
- Oil for frying

INSTRUCTIONS

1. Season with soy sauce or salt and steam for 5 minutes, or until the fish is cooked through and flaky. Fish may be cooked any way you desire, as long as the fish doesn't have a burnt crispy coating on it (poach, bake, even stir-fry in a pan on low heat). The fish will be easier to handle if it has cooled down a bit.

2. Make the mango salad while the fish is resting and chilling. There should be no large bits of Thai chilies left in the mortar, then add the palm sugar and crush until the mixture is smooth. The sugar should be completely dissolved by the time you add fish sauce and lime juice. Add the mango, shallots, and dried shrimp to a bowl and mix well. While the fish is frying, allow to sit for a few minutes.

3. Transfer the fish to a muslin-lined bowl after it has cooled enough to handle. Push the fish as hard as you can to remove as much liquid as possible (this is why it's important to let the fish cool first; if it's too warm, you won't want to squeeze as hard!).

4. You may use a mortar and pestle to pulverize the fish into a powdery consistency.

5. In a wok or deep pot, heat about 1 - 1.5 inches of oil over high heat to 400°F, and be sure to read and follow the safety instructions above!! Use a broad saucepan or wok to make folding the fish simpler, so you can get to it more

quickly. If you have a 9-inch saucepan, you may make two batches of fried fish with this recipe's ingredients.

6. At this point, you may add roughly half of your fish and watch it bubble vigorously. Clean the fish's edges with a skimmer, then fried the fish until it's golden brown. To help the fish brown more evenly, I sometimes submerge the top of the fish. The fish can be folded into a half-circle or other form after it's golden brown, but it's not required. Lift the fish out of the oil with a slotted skimmer and shake it several times to remove the oil that has accumulated in the fish's internal cavity. Drain on a piece of paper towel.

7. Serve the fish with roasted peanuts on a serving platter. Serve the mango salad with the fish with chopped cilantro. Jasmine rice is a good accompaniment. Enjoy!

13. TAMARIND PRAWN CURRY

Prep: 5 mins

Cook: 15 mins

Easy

Serves 2

INGREDIENTS

- 1 tbsp vegetable oil
- 1 onion, chopped
- 1 red chilli, finely chopped
- 2 garlic cloves, crushed
- 1 tbsp grated ginger
- 1 tsp turmeric
- 1 tsp cumin seeds
- 1 tsp ground coriander
- 400g can cherry tomatoes
- 1-2 tbsp tamarind paste (see tip, below)
- 250g raw king prawns
- 250g cooked basmati rice
- handful of coriander leaves, to serve

INSTRUCTIONS

1. In a medium-sized frying pan, heat the oil and sauté the onion for 5-8 minutes, or until the onion is translucent. Spices should be added after another minute of frying the vegetables. Toss the cherry tomatoes into the pan, along with the can of water that has been swirled out.

2. When the tomatoes begin to burst and the sauce thickens, cook for another 5 minutes. For 2-3 minutes till the prawns are cooked after adding tamarind and prawns, simmer. Coriander can be sprinkled on top of this dish as well as the curry.

14. THAI STEAMED MUSSELS

Prep: 20 mins

Cook: 10 mins

Total: 30 mins

Yield: 6 servings

INGREDIENTS

- 5 pounds fresh mussels, scrubbed and debearded
- ⅓ cup fresh lime juice
- 1 (13.5 ounce) can unsweetened coconut milk
- ⅓ cup dry white wine
- 1 ½ tablespoons Thai red curry paste
- 1 ½ tablespoons minced garlic
- 1 tablespoon Asian fish sauce
- 1 tablespoon white sugar
- 2 cups chopped fresh cilantro

INSTRUCTIONS

1. Add the lime juice, coconut milk, wine, curry paste, garlic, fish sauce, and sugar to a large stock pot and bring to a boil. Bring the mixture to a boil over high heat, stirring frequently to dissolve the sugar and curry paste. Add mussels after 2 minutes of boiling. Cover and simmer for

5 to 8 minutes, stirring periodically, until the mussels open.

2. Discard any mussels that have not opened. Toss the cilantro with the mussels and their liquor in a serving dish.

15.SARDINE AND LEMONGRASS SALAD

Yield: serves 2 people

Time: 10 minutes

INGREDIENTS

- 2 tbsp. Thai sweet chile sauce
- 1 tbsp. fresh lime juice
- 1/2 tsp. kosher salt
- 1 piece lemongrass, tough outer leaves discarded, inner core thinly sliced
- 1 3 3/4-oz can sardines in water, drained, and cut into 1-inch pieces
- 1 1/2 cups cups lightly packed torn cilantro leaves and stems
- 1/2 small red onion, thinly sliced

INSTRUCTIONS

1. Mix the lime juice and salt into the sweet chile sauce in a big basin. Serve with lime wedges or lemon slices on the side for spicing up the dish. Serve the salad on a dish as soon as possible.

16.PEPPERY GARLIC SHRIMP

PREP TIME: 10 mins

COOK TIME: 5 mins

MARINATING: 60 mins

TOTAL TIME: 75 mins

INGREDIENTS

- 4 cloves garlic, crushed
- 1/2 teaspoon salt
- 1 teaspoon crushed black peppercorns
- 1 teaspoon freshly squeezed lemon juice
- 2 tablespoons brandy
- 1 pound medium shrimp, shelled and deveined
- 1 to 2 tablespoons extra virgin olive oil
- 2 tablespoons chopped fresh parsley

INSTRUCTIONS

Marinate the shrimp:

1. Crushed garlic, salt, peppercorns, lemon juice, and brandy should all be combined. Make sure to marinate the shrimp for at least an hour, if not more, and up to overnight.

Sauté the shrimp:

1. Add olive oil to a large, heavy pan and heat over medium-high heat. Serve immediately, tossing often with the shrimp. Cooking shrimp takes less time if they have marinated for a longer period of time.

2. Serve when the shrimp is opaque in the center (generally only 2-3 minutes).
3. Add chopped parsley to the dish as a finishing touch.

17.TILAPIA IN THAI SAUCE

Prep: 20 mins

Cook: 10 mins

Serves 2

INGREDIENTS

- 4 tilapia fillets
- 2 tbsp cornflour
- 2 tbsp sunflower oil
- 4 spring onions , sliced
- 2 garlic cloves , crushed
- small piece fresh ginger , finely chopped
- 2 tbsp soy sauce
- 1 tbsp brown sugar
- juice 1 lime , plus 1 lime chopped into wedges, to serve
- 1 red chilli , deseeded and sliced
- handful Thai basil leaves or coriander leaves

INSTRUCTIONS

1. Set the fish fillets aside after coating them with cornflour. Crispy-skinned fish fillets are ready when they sizzle for 2-3 minutes on each side in a big non-stick frying pan that has been heated to a high temperature. Add the soy sauce,

brown sugar, and lime juice to the same pan and bring to a boil, then reduce the heat and simmer for a few minutes. Serve the fish with lime wedges and a dollop of the sauce, garnished with chilli, Thai basil, or coriander.

18.THAI BANANA SALSA WITH KING PRAWNS

Prep: 15 mins

Cook: 3 mins

Additional: 7 mins

Total: 25 mins

Yield: 4 servings

INGREDIENTS

- 2 bananas, peeled and thinly sliced
- 2 cucumbers - peeled, seeded, and diced
- ½ cup fresh mint leaves
- ½ cup fresh cilantro leaves
- 1 teaspoon finely chopped fresh ginger root
- 1 fresh red chile pepper, thinly sliced
- ¼ cup lime juice
- 1 tablespoon fish sauce
- 1 tablespoon brown sugar
- 1 ½ pounds tiger prawns, peeled and deveined

INSTRUCTIONS

1. Salad is a great way to get a variety of fresh vegetables into your diet.
2. Pour the lime juice, fish sauce, and the brown sugar into a small bowl and mix until the sugar is completely dissolved. Make sure the salsa is thoroughly mixed in.
3. A big pot of lightly salted water should be brought to a rolling boil before you begin. Cook the prawns for three minutes or until the meat is opaque when you put them in the water. Serve alongside the banana salsa.

19. THAI-STYLE BEEF WITH BASIL AND CHILIES (PHAT BAI HORAPHA)

Active: 15 mins

Total: 30 mins

Serves: 2 to 3 servings

INGREDIENTS

- 1 pound (450g) flank steak, skirt steak, hanger steak, or flap meat, cut into 1/4-inch-thick strips
- 1 tablespoon (15ml) soy sauce, divided
- 5 teaspoons (25ml) Asian fish sauce, divided
- 1 teaspoon (4g) white sugar
- 4 to 6 fresh red or green Thai bird chilies, divided
- 6 medium cloves garlic, divided
- 1 1/2 tablespoons (20g) palm sugar (see note)
- 1 small shallot, thinly sliced
- 4 makrut lime leaves, very thinly sliced into hairs (central vein discarded), plus more for garnish (see note)
- 2 tablespoons (30ml) vegetable or canola oil, divided
- 2 cups packed Thai purple basil (about 2 ounces; 55g)(see note)
- Dried Thai chili flakes or red pepper flakes to taste (optional)
- 1/4 cup fried shallots (see note)
- Kosher salt
- Cooked rice, for serving

INSTRUCTIONS

1. Combine beef, 1 teaspoon soy sauce, 2 teaspoons fish sauce, and white sugar in a bowl. Toss to combine and set in refrigerator to marinate for at least 15 minutes and up to overnight.
2. How to Make Quick and Easy Zucchini-Basil Soup
3. Place half of the Thai chilies and garlic in a stone mortar with palm sugar and mash until smooth. Pestle the mixture until it resembles a smooth paste. In a mortar and pestle, mix together the remaining fish sauce and soy sauce. Set away for a later time. In a small dish, mix the remaining garlic and chiles with the shallot and lime leaves.
4. In a wok or frying pan, heat 1 tablespoon of oil until shimmering and smoking before beginning to cook. A minute later, add half of the steak and cook it without moving. When the meat is somewhat cooked but still pink in parts, continue swirling and tossing for another minute or so. Make a big basin for it all. Transfer the remaining steak to the same bowl and repeat the process with another tablespoon of oil and the remaining meat. Clean the wok.
5. reheat wok and add all meat, garlic/chili/makrut lime combination over high heat. After approximately a minute, the stir-fry should be fragrant and the shallots have softened fully.
6. Wok-cooking: Add sauce mixture to wok and stir regularly to decrease. As long as the meat appears wet, but the bottom of the pan is dry, it's done cooking. Add basil and stir to mix immediately. Optional Thai chili or red chili flakes can be added to the salt and pepper to taste. Place on a serving plate and serve immediately.

Garnish with fried shallots and additional makrut lime strands. Serve with rice right away.

SPECIAL EQUIPMENT

1. Mortar and pestle (see note), wok

20.THAI PORK DUMPLINGS

Preparation: 30 min

Cook: 15 min

Clean up: 15 min

Steps: 4 steps

INGREDIENTS

Cilantro Paste:

- ½ bunch fresh cilantro
- (stems removed)
- ½ tbsp brown sugar
- ½ tbsp grated ginger
- 1 tsp black pepper
- 1 tsp pureed garlic
- 1 tbsp fish sauce

meat paste:

- 1 bundle bean threads
- (tang hoon)
- 300 g ground pork
- 1 tbsp fish sauce
- 1 tsp pureed garlic

- 1 tbsp cornstarch
- 1 packet wonton wrappers
- 10 cups chicken stock
- 1 stalk lemongrass
- (sliced, chopped; bulb and tough outer leaves removed)
- 3-5 shitake mushrooms
- (sliced)
- 1 scallion
- (thinly sliced)
- ½ bunch cilantro
- (leaves only)

INSTRUCTIONS

Make cilantro paste

1. Using a mortar and pestle or a blender, combine the first six ingredients and process until a smooth paste forms. Set away for a later time.

Soak bean thread

1. For around 15 minutes, soak the bean thread in boiling water to make it translucent.
2. When bean thread are finished soaking, drain. Rough cut noodles into 3" lengths.

Make dumplings

1. Gather the ingredients for dumplings and mix them together in a bowl: ground pork, garlic, fish sauce, and cornstarch.
2. Spread out six wonton wrappers on a clean, dry work area. Dip your fingers or a brush into a basin of water to get the job done.

3. Each wrapper should have 1 tsp of filling in the centre.
4. Wet the outer edges of the first wrapper with your fingertips or a brush to help it stick.
5. Repeat for the remaining filling.

Make broth

1. Add chicken stock to a soup pot and bring it to a boil. Lemongrass can be added. Simmer for 5 minutes after coming to a boil.
2. Cook the dumplings and mushrooms in the broth. The dumplings should be floating rather than sinking after 5 minutes of boiling.
3. Noodles made from bean threads can be added.
4. Add the paste and adjust the spices with salt and pepper.

21.PORK BELLY DRUNKEN NOODLES

PREP TIME: 10 minutes

COOK TIME: 10 minutes

SERVES: 2

INGREDIENTS

- 5 garlic cloves, roughly chopped
- 3 birds' eye chillies, roughly chopped
- 1 large yellow chilli, roughly chopped
- 2 tbsp vegetable oil or the rendered fat from the pork belly
- 200g (7 oz) skinless pork belly, sliced into thin strips
- 1 cup sliced Asian greens e.g. Chinese broccoli, Chinese kale, pak chok, bok choy

- 300g (10.5 oz) fresh rice noodles*
- 4 tbsp oyster sauce
- 1 tbsp fish sauce
- 1 tsp dark soy sauce
- 1 ½ tsp white sugar
- 1 heaped cup Thai holy basil*

INSTRUCTIONS

1. You'll need a mortar and pestle to grind up the garlic and chilies into a coarse mixture.
2. Add the oil or pig fat to a wok or frying pan and bring it to a boil. Stir-fry the chili paste for 30 seconds after adding it to the pan with the rest of the ingredients. Stir-fry the pork until it is almost done. After 1 minute, add the Asian greens and continue to cook until the greens are soft and the pork is done. When you're done with the noodles and all of the other condiments, add the sugar. Toss everything together in a pan and cook for a few minutes.
3. Toss in the basil once the heat has been turned off. Serve hot.

22.THAI-STYLE GRILLED PORK SKEWERS (MOO PING) RECIPE

Active: 30 mins

Total: 4 hrs 30 mins

Serves: 4 to 6 servings

INGREDIENTS

- 4 medium cloves garlic (20g), minced
- 2 tablespoons (15g) minced cilantro stems, plus fresh cilantro leaves for serving
- 2 tablespoons (30g) finely chopped palm sugar (see note)
- 1 tablespoon (15ml) fish sauce
- 1 tablespoon (15ml) soy sauce
- 1 tablespoon (15ml) oyster sauce
- 1 1/2 teaspoons (6g) ground white pepper
- 1/2 teaspoon (2g) MSG powder (optional)
- 2 pounds (900g) pork butt, in one piece
- 1 (5 1/2-ounce; 160ml) can unsweetened coconut cream (see note)
- 1 recipe Thai Dried Chili-Vinegar Dipping Sauce, for serving (optional)

INSTRUCTIONS

1. Mix together garlic, cilantro stems, and palm sugar in a small bowl. Add fish sauce, soy sauce, oyster sauce (and MSG if using), and white pepper to taste. Set away for a later time.
2. For 15 minutes and up to 30 minutes, put pork in the freezer (partially freezing the pork makes it easier to slice). Slice pork against the grain into 2-inch-long, 1-

inch-wide, and 1/8-inch-thick strips with a sharp chef's knife or slicing knife. Slice the pig butt into 2-inch wide by 1-inch thick chunks, then cut those chunks into 1/8-inch-thick strips crosswise for the most efficient method.

3. Toss the pork with the marinade in a large basin until the meat is completely covered. Refrigerate for at least four hours, and up to 36 hours, carefully wrapped in plastic.

4. Assemble an accordion of pork by threading a piece of pork onto a skewer and piercing it twice to fasten it. A 2-inch handle and pointed tip are the only things visible on this skewer, so continue to thread pork onto it, ensuring sure it is securely bundled together. The leftover pork should be skewered in the same manner.

5. The space between bricks should be adjusted to the length of your skewered food. Light a charcoal-filled chimney. In order to equally distribute the coals, pour out the charcoal and spread it out in between the bricks.

6. With handles overhanging the brick closest to you and tips balancing on a brick wall further away, place skewers straight over a hot coal, on top of bricks. Apply coconut cream on meat using a brush. Pork skewers should be roasted for 8 to 10 minutes on each side, turning them periodically and coating them with coconut cream to keep the meat from burning. If you notice any flare-ups, you should move the skewers around to get them away from the flames. Rest for 1 to 2 minutes on the serving dish before serving. It is best to serve the dish right away with lime wedges, cilantro and a dipping sauce (if desired).

SPECIAL EQUIPMENT

1. Grill, chimney starter, bricks, bamboo skewers

23.THAI WATERFALL BEEF SALAD - A FEAST OF FLAVOR!

Prep: 20 mins

Cook: 12 mins

Total: 32 mins

Servings: 2 servings

INGREDIENTS

- 1 to 2 sirloin steaks, depending on the amount of meat you prefer

Marinade:

- 2 tablespoons oyster sauce
- 2 tablespoons soy sauce
- 1 tablespoon lime juice, or lemon juice
- 2 tablespoons brown sugar

For Salad:

- 6 cups salad greens
- 1 cup bean sprouts
- 1 handful mint, or basil, fresh, lightly chopped or torn
- 1 cup coriander, fresh
- 1 cup papaya, fresh, cubed or cut into spears
- 1 cup tomatoes, cherry, left whole or sliced in half

Dressing:

- 1 to 2 tablespoons fish sauce, available at Asian food stores
- 3 tablespoons lime juice, or lemon juice
- 1 1/2 tablespoons soy sauce
- 1/2 teaspoon cayenne pepper
- 1 teaspoon brown sugar
- 2 tablespoons rice, sticky variety, toasted and ground, OR 2 tablespoons ground peanuts

INSTRUCTIONS

1. To begin, gather all of the necessary components.
2. The sugar in the marinade can be dissolved by swirling it into the contents in a cup or basin. Pour over the meat and turn to coat. Marinate in the refrigerator for a few hours.
3. There is a substitution for peanuts in this recipe: Fry 2 tbsp. of uncooked sticky rice over medium-high heat in a dry frying pan. Dry-fry the rice until it begins to pop and is slightly toasted, stirring constantly. To ground the cooked rice into a fine powder, remove it from the pan and wait for it to cool before using a coffee grinder or pestle and mortar.
4. In a cup or mixing dish, combine all of the dressing ingredients and whisk until the sugar melts (adjust fish sauce according to your desired level of saltiness). Then, assemble your salad components, including greens and other greens.
5. Turn the steak only once or twice on a hot grill to keep the juices in (meat should still be pink in the center).
6. If using an oven to cook the steak: Make sure your oven is on the broil setting. On a baking sheet lined with foil or

parchment paper, place the steak. On the second-to-highest ring of the oven, place the dish. When the steak is done on the exterior but still a little pink on the inside, broil it for 5 to 7 minutes on each side.

7. Make a dressing for the salad while the steak is cooking. Add extra fish sauce or lime juice if the dish is too salty for your liking.

8. When the salad is ready to be served, divide it into individual servings. If you can, slice the steak as thinly as you possibly can, then pile on the sirloin. Enjoy!

24.BEEF SATAY WITH THAI PEANUT SAUCE

Prep Time: 15 mins

Cook Time: 15 mins

Marinating: 1 d

Total Time: 1 d 30 mins

INGREDIENTS

- 13-16 bamboo skewers , 16cm / 6.5" long (Note 1)

Marinade:

- 600g / 1.2lb beef rump steak (top sirloin in the US) , 2.5 cm/1" pieces (Note 2)
- 1/4 cup coconut mik , full fat (I use Ayam, Note 3)
- 1 tbsp curry powder (Note 4)
- 1 tsp white sugar
- 2 tsp red curry paste (Note 5)
- 1/2 tsp baking soda / bi-carb (tenderiser, Note 6)
- 1 tsp salt

Thai Peanut Sauce:

- 1 tbsp red curry paste (Note 5)
- 2/3 cup coconut milk , full fat (I use Ayam, Note 3)
- 1/3 cup natural peanut butter , smooth (Note 7)
- 1 1/2 tbsp white sugar
- 1 tsp dark soy sauce (Note 8)
- 1/2 tsp salt
- 1 tbsp cider vinegar (Note 9)
- 1/3 cup water

Cooking & Serving:

- 1 1/2 tbsp vegetable oil , for cooking
- 2 tbsp peanuts , finely chopped
- Lime wedges (optional)
- Coriander / cilantro leaves and sliced red chilli (optional)

INSTRUCTIONS

1. Skewers should be soaked in water for two hours before cooking on a grill or over charcoal.

Thai Beef Satay Skewers:

1. In a bowl, combine the meat and marinade. Marinate overnight in cling wrap (do not reduce marinating time else the beef may not tenderise enough).
2. Assemble four pieces on each skewer.
3. In a large nonstick pan, heat 1.5 tbsp of oil over medium-high heat.
4. Cook for a full 10 minutes: Skewers should be fried in batches for 2 to 2 1/2 minutes on all four sides until they are deep brown and cooked through. Note: Baking soda tenderized meat must be cooked completely to become

tender. A little bit of chewiness remains if the meat is medium or less.)

5. Skewers should be served with Peanut Sauce after resting for 3 minutes on a platter.

Thai Peanut Sauce:

1. In a small saucepan, combine all the ingredients for the Peanut Sauce and warm gently.
2. Stir everything together and cook for 5 minutes, stirring occasionally. Water can be used to fine-tune the sauce's viscosity - it should be pourable yet thick.
3. Keep the skewers warm by removing the pot from the burner and covering it with a lid.

Serving:

1. Pour the sauce into a basin. Add some chopped peanuts and mix them in if you want.
2. Stack the skewers and garnish with remaining peanuts, coriander, and chilli on a serving plate.
3. Serve with a dipping sauce on the side. Make the dinner complete by serving it with a side of Jasmine Rice, Thai Fried rice, or Pineapple Fried rice.

25.LAMB CUTLETS WITH THAI STYLE DRESSING

Serves: 4

Prep: 10m

NOTE: + 15 mins marinating & 5 mins resting time

Cooking: 10m

INGREDIENTS

- 1 tbs drained green peppercorns
- 1/3 cup (80ml) lime juice
- 2 tbs fish sauce
- 2 tbs brown sugar
- 1 tsp sesame oil
- 5cm-piece ginger, cut into matchsticks
- 1 long red chilli, finely chopped (optional)
- 12 Coles Australian Lamb Cutlets
- 2 Lebanese cucumbers, thinly sliced
- 350g mixed tomatoes, halved
- 1 red onion, thinly sliced
- 1 cup coriander leaves
- 1 cup mint leaves
- 1/2 cup (75g) cashews, toasted, coarsely chopped

INSTRUCTIONS

1. The peppercorns, lime juice, fish sauce, sugar, oil and ginger, if using can be combined in a large glass or ceramic bowl. In a small dish, put aside half of the dressing. Turn the lamb in the remaining dressing and serve. Allow the flavors to meld for 15 minutes before serving.

2. A barbeque grill or chargrill should be preheated to medium-high heat. Drain the meat. For medium-rare, heat for 2-3 minutes on each side. Transfer to a serving platter or bowl. Wrap it up with foil. Rest for five minutes.
3. Serve the cucumber, tomato, onion, coriander, and mint on a serving plate. Sprinkle cashews on top. Put the lamb on a serving plate. Reserving some of the dressing, serve on the side.

26. BEEF AND BROCCOLI – THAI STYLE

Prep Time: 10 minutes

Cook Time: 15 minutes

Servings: 2

Calories: 513kcal

INGREDIENTS

The sauce

- 1 tbsp soy sauce – Thai light soy sauce or Golden Mountain sauce
- 1 tbsp fish sauce
- 2 tsp oyster sauce – Thai oyster sauce
- 1 tsp dark soy – Thai sweet soy (or substitute a big pinch of sugar)
- 1 tsp sambal oelek or garlic chili sauce
- 3 tbsp water

Beef and broccoli

- 12 oz beef sirloin sliced thinly across the grain. Alternately, you can slice up a flank or skirt steak.
- 12 oz broccolini or gai lan if you can get it, cut into large pieces
- 1 medium onion thinly sliced (optional but tasty)
- 2 tsp garlic ginger paste
- 1/2 tsp cornstarch
- 2 tsp water mixed with the 1/2 tsp cornstarch
- 3 tbsp neutral oil you might need a bit more. Don't skimp. Saving a few calories is not worth it here.
- 1-2 red chilies thinly sliced (optional)
- sesame seeds to garnish

INSTRUCTIONS

1. Restaurants use burners that are only slightly colder than the sun to accomplish high-heat stir-fry methods. Because you don't have this (at least, not yet), putting in a little additional effort is a necessary evil in this situation.
2. In a small bowl, mix together the sauce ingredients. Set away for a later time.
3. Set up your meat. Sirloin steaks can be cut into a tiny roast (or "baseball steak"). Slice the sirloin as thinly as possible (1/8") across the grain after freezing it for about 20 minutes. You can use a vertical bias if you're employing a flank or a skirt slice (so the slice is bigger than the steak is high).
4. If you have a wok, use it for this if you have one available. Basically, it's easier. You may also use a large frying pan. It should be preheated at medium-high heat. The oil should be added in a quantity of 2 tablespoons at this point.

5. It is time to raise the thermostat. It's time to crank it up. When the oil begins to shimmer, add half of the steak and stir. Half the battle is won. You don't want to fill your pan to the brim. The steak won't brown and you'll get steam if you grill it that way. Toss regularly while cooking until it turns a darker shade of brown. Remove.

6. Add the final tablespoon of olive oil to the mix. Cook the second half of the meat the same way you did the first. Set away for a later time.

7. To reduce the temperature, lower it to medium-low. At this stage, if your wok appears dry, add a little additional oil. Cook the onions until they are tender and translucent, about 5 minutes.

8. Add a bit more heat. Stir-fry the broccolini until it begins to soften, then remove it from the pan. Be active. Make a mess of things. As if you were a celebrity. Make the most of it. Depending on how high your heat is, this might take anything from a few minutes to a few hours.

9. Try to achieve a little bit of that burnt flavor on the broccolini while cooking. It's time to go for it. Your onions will begin to shrink and turn a darker shade of brown. Fried shallots in a dish. There you go. Add a couple of tablespoons of water to the pan if the onions begin to brown after approximately two minutes.

10. Add the paste of garlic and ginger to the pan and lower the heat. Add the steak back into the wok and cook for another 30 seconds.

11. Add the sauce and mix until the food is heated thoroughly. Sit back and wait for your sauce to thicken a little bit before adding your cornstarch-water combination and broccolini. Taste. Let it cook for an additional minute if you believe it's not salty enough. Remove from the heat. If using, add the red chilies.

12. Serve with jasmine rice and sesame seeds as a garnish.

27.PORK & HOLY BASIL STIR-FRY

PREP: 10 minutes

COOK: 5 minutes

TOTAL: 15 minutes

INGREDIENTS

- 3 tablespoons vegetable oil
- 2 shallots (thinly sliced)
- 7 cloves garlic (sliced)
- 3 Thai bird or holland chilies (de-seeded, if desired, and thinly sliced)
- 1 pound ground pork (450g)
- 1 teaspoon sugar
- 1 tablespoon fish sauce
- 1 tablespoon thin/light soy sauce
- 2 teaspoons dark soy sauce
- 2 teaspoons oyster sauce
- ⅓ cup low sodium chicken broth or water
- holy basil leaves (about 1 1/2 cups packed)

INSTRUCTIONS

1. Pour in the oil, shallots, and garlic, and cook for 3 minutes over medium-high heat. After another minute, add the chiles. Grease and cook the skillet over high heat, stirring occasionally, until the ground pork is crisp-tender.
2. Sweeten to taste with a teaspoon of honey or agave nectar. Deglaze the pan with the broth or water and

continue to stir-fry for another minute. The liquid should evaporate fast because your pan is on a high heat. Stir-fry the basil until wilted. Serve with rice.

28. THAI BASIL MINCED PORK

Prep time: 10 mins

Cook time: 6 mins

Total time: 16 mins

INGREDIENTS

- 1 cup ground pork
- ⅓ cup diced red bell pepper
- ⅓ cup diced green bell pepper
- ⅓ cup diced onion
- 4 cloves garlic, minced
- 1 handful of fresh Thai basil leaves
- half a lime, optional
- 3 tablespoons oil
- 1 tablespoon fish sauce
- 1 teaspoon soy sauce
- 1 teaspoon sugar

INSTRUCTIONS

1. Add the ground pork to a medium-sized skillet and cook for 2-3 minutes, or until the meat has turned a darker shade of brown. Remove the pork from the pan and put it aside (leave oil in the pan).

2. For 1-2 minutes, sauté garlic in olive oil until aromatic. Then add green, red, and onion and stir fry for another minute or so.
3. Toss the Thai basil leaves into the pan with the meat.
4. Add fish sauce, soy sauce, and sugar, then cook for one minute over medium-high heat.
5. Serve with lime juice drizzled over top.

29. GARLIC LOVERS THAI BASIL CHICKEN

INGREDIENTS

Thai Basil Chicken Stir Fry:

- 1 ½ pound chicken breasts, chopped into small pieces (see notes)
- 12 cloves garlic
- 4-12 birds eye chilies (see notes)
- 1 shallot, finely minced
- 1 tablespoon oil
- 2 cups holy basil

Sauce:

- 3 tablespoons light soy sauce
- 1 tablespoon oyster sauce
- 2 tablespoons golden mountain sauce
- 2 teaspoons fish sauce
- 1 tablespoon sugar
- ½ teaspoon black pepper

INSTRUCTIONS

PULSE:

1. Break down the garlic and the bird's eye chilies in a mortar and pestle by putting them together in the container. Set aside if you prefer to use a food processor or a small spice grinder.

SAUCE:

1. In a small dish, combine the sauce ingredients together with 3 tablespoons water; leave aside.

BASIL CHICKEN:

1. On medium-high heat in a pan, saute the minced shallot and minced chile for about a minute or so, then add the chicken. Using a wooden spoon, crumble the chicken like you would ground beef and cook for 3-4 minutes. Pour in the sauce and mix it up with a spoon. Let it simmer for a minute or two until the basil begins to soften, then remove it from the heat and serve. Remove from the fire and serve immediately with a side of jasmine rice and a sprinkle of sesame seeds.

30. THAI FRIED CHICKEN

Equipment:

1. Large Pot & Slotted Spoon (for deep frying)
2. Pestle & Mortar (see notes for sub)
3. Large Mixing Bowl & Cling Film (for marinating)
4. Medium Mixing Bowl (for dredging)
5. Sharp Knife & Chopping Board
6. Paper Towels
7. Kitchen Thermometer
8. Cooling Rack

INGREDIENTS

Marinade

- 2.5lb / 1.2kg bone in skin on Chicken Pieces, patted dry with paper towels (drumsticks and thighs work best)
- 5 cloves of Garlic, peeled
- 1/4 cup roughly chopped Coriander/Cilantro Roots & Stems, washed as necessary (see notes)
- 1 tbsp Light Soy Sauce
- 2 tsp Oyster Sauce
- 1 tsp Sugar
- 1/2 tsp EACH: Salt, White Pepper, Black Pepper

Batter

- 1 cup / 128g Tempura Batter (see notes)
- 3/4 cup / 180ml COLD Soda Water
- 1 tsp Chicken Boullion Powder/Oxo Cube
- 1-2 Ice Cubes (optional)
- 3-4 cups / 750ml-1litre Vegetable Oil, for deep frying

To Serve

- 4 Shallots, finely & evenly diced (to make crispy shallots)
- Sticky Rice
- Thai Sweet Chilli Sauce

INSTRUCTIONS

1. Mix together 5 garlic cloves, 1/4 cup coarsely chopped coriander/cilantro roots and stems, 1 tsp sugar, and white and black pepper in a pestle and mortar. Then grind the mixture into a fine powder. Make a smooth paste by grinding.

2. Add 1 tbsp soy sauce and 2 tsp oyster sauce to a large mixing bowl and mix thoroughly. With your hands, toss in the chicken pieces and coat well. The meat should be well coated in the marinade. Cling wrap the top and put it in the fridge for an hour or so. As long as you have the time, marinate for at least four hours (best results over night).

3. Place the shallots between two paper towels while you prepare the rest of the dish. Squeeze out as much wetness as possible by pressing down firmly with your palms. Set aside for now.

4. Add your shallots to a saucepan of oil that has been heated to 120C/250F. The goal is to keep the temperature low and gradual so that as much moisture as possible may be extracted, resulting in a crispy result. Sautee over medium-high heat until the onions begin to darken in color, about 5 minutes. In a matter of seconds, they go from beautiful to burned. Remove the food from the pan and place it on a sheet of paper towels.

5. Bring the oil to a temperature of 175 degrees Celsius/350 degrees Fahrenheit. Combine the tempura batter and the chicken powder in a medium-sized mixing bowl. The

lumps should be smoothed out by adding COLD soda water and stirring. You're looking for something that's thick and creamy like double or heavy cream. Carefully lower a piece of chicken into the oil after coating it with the batter. To get the best results, you'll need to work in batches of three or four. To keep the batter cool, I normally add an ice cube to the mixture. A cooler environment results in crispier chicken.

6. Maintain the temperature at 165C/330F, and you'll be OK; just keep it there. Each side should take around 5-8 minutes depending on how large the chicken pieces are. Keep warm on a cooling rack with paper towels beneath it after cooking. Your goal is for the outside of the chicken to be browned and crispy, while the inside remains boiling hot (internal temperature 165F/75C). If you're feeling a little worn out, check out the notes.

7. Add a final sprinkle of salt (optional) to the chicken before serving with crispy shallots on top and a sweet chilli sauce on the side. Enjoy!

31.CREAMY COCONUT LIME CHICKEN

INGREDIENTS

- 4-6 boneless, skinless chicken breasts
- Salt and pepper
- 1 tablespoon olive oil
- 1/2 cup diced onion
- 1 red bell pepper, diced
- 2-3 cloves garlic, minced
- 1 cup chicken stock
- 1 tablespoon cornstarch
- 1/4 teaspoon red chili flakes
- 1/2 teaspoon turmeric
- 1 (13.6 oz.) can coconut milk
- 2 tablespoons lime juice
- 1/2 cup heavy cream
- 1-2 tablespoons chopped fresh cilantro

INSTRUCTIONS

1. Salt and pepper the chicken before cooking it. In a large skillet, heat the oil to medium-high heat. Toss in the chicken breasts and cook for 5-7 minutes on each side, or until they're golden brown and cooked through. Make a serving and cover with a lid to keep it warm.
2. Simmer for around 5 minutes or until the veggies begin to soften before removing from the heat.
3. In a small saucepan, combine the chicken stock and cornstarch and bring to a boil over medium heat. Add the red chili flakes and turmeric to the pan. The sauce will

thicken as it simmers, so keep an eye on it and stir frequently.

4. Simmer for another 3 to 5 minutes before adding the coconut milk. Return the chicken to the pan and stir in the lime juice and cream. Salt and pepper to taste, if necessary. Chicken should be cooked through in another 5 to 10 minutes at this point. Before serving, sprinkle the dish with a generous amount of chopped cilantro.

32. THIS CLASSIC THAI CHICKEN FRIED RICE IS SIMPLE YET TASTY

Prep: 15 mins

Cook: 15 mins

Total: 30 mins

Yield: 6 cups

INGREDIENTS

- 4 to 5 cups cooked rice, preferably several days old
- 1 boneless, skinless chicken breast, or 2 thighs, chopped into small pieces
- 3 tablespoons soy sauce
- 3 tablespoons chicken stock
- 3 tablespoons fish sauce, more to taste
- 1 tablespoon lime juice, more to taste
- 1 teaspoon granulated sugar
- 1/8 teaspoon white pepper, or black pepper
- 2 to 3 tablespoons vegetable oil
- 4 spring onions, sliced, white and green parts separated
- 3 to 4 cloves garlic, minced

- 1 red or green chile pepper, thinly sliced, or a sprinkling of chile flakes
- 5 to 7 fresh shiitake mushrooms, stemmed and chopped into small pieces
- 1 small stalk celery, thinly sliced
- 1/2 cup frozen peas
- 1 large egg
- Thai sweet chile sauce, for serving, optional

INSTRUCTIONS

1. Gather the ingredients.
2. You can separate clumps of cold leftover rice by drizzling a teaspoon or two of oil on your fingertips and working your way through it.
3. Add 1 tablespoon of soy sauce to the chopped chicken in a bowl. Set aside to cool.
4. Combine the chicken stock, fish sauce, lime juice, sugar, and white pepper with the remaining 2 tablespoons of soy sauce. Set away for a later time.
5. A wok or a big frying pan should be heated to high or medium-high heat, depending on your preference. Swirl in 2 tablespoons of oil before adding the spring onion whites, garlic and chile to the pan.
6. Stir-fry the chicken for a minute, then add the rest of the ingredients. 2 to 3 minutes of stirring or until chicken is opaque throughout.
7. For 2 to 3 minutes, add the mushrooms and celery and continue to stir-fry until all of the ingredients are cooked through (celery should stay a little crunchy). If your pan or wok gets too dry, you may always add a little extra oil.
8. Add the rice while the heat is still on. Gently raise and swirl the rice in a stir-fry using a spatula or other flat tool.

9. Add 1 to 2 teaspoons of the stir-fry sauce at a time. Once all the sauce has been added, stir-fry for another 6 to 10 minutes until everything is heated through.
10. Stir in the frozen peas until they are well-coated. Push the rest of the pan's contents to the side to reveal the pan's center.
11. Stir-fry the scrambled egg as soon as it's cracked.
12. After 2 minutes of high-heat stirring, the rice should be light and readily separate into individual grains.
13. Remove from the fire and taste; if necessary, add a bit more fish sauce. Lime juice can be used if the dish is overly salty. Serve with green onion slices that have been cut up but not used. Serve with Thai chile sauce on the side for those who want it extra hot.

33. CLASSIC SESAME NOODLES WITH CHICKEN

Total: 20 mins

Servings: 4

INGREDIENTS

- 8 ounces whole-wheat spaghetti
- 3 tablespoons toasted (dark) sesame oil
- 2 scallions, chopped
- 1 tablespoon minced garlic
- 2 teaspoons minced fresh ginger
- 1 teaspoon brown sugar
- 2 tablespoons reduced-sodium soy sauce
- 2 tablespoons ketchup
- 8 ounces cooked boneless, skinless chicken breast, shredded

- 1 cup julienned carrots
- 1 cup sliced snap peas
- 3 tablespoons toasted sesame seeds

INSTRUCTIONS

1. In a saucepan of boiling water, cook the spaghetti according to the package instructions. Pour into a large dish and rinse well.
2. Then add the sesame oil, scallions and garlic to a small saucepan and bring it to a boil. When it begins to sizzle, turn the heat down to medium. Toss in the garlic and cook for another 15 seconds. Toss with soy sauce and ketchup after taking the dish off of the stove. Mix all ingredients except sesame seeds and chicken in a large bowl and toss to combine.

34. THAI CHICKEN BALLS

Prep: 20 mins

Cook: 40 mins

Total: 1 hr

Servings: 8

Yield: 30 balls

INGREDIENTS

- 2 pounds ground chicken
- 1 cup dry bread crumbs
- 4 green onions, sliced
- 1 tablespoon ground coriander seed
- 1 cup chopped fresh cilantro
- ¼ cup sweet chili sauce

- 2 tablespoons fresh lemon juice
- oil for frying

INSTRUCTIONS

1. Mix the bread crumbs and chicken in a large basin. Squeeze lemon juice into the mixture and season with chili sauce and green onion.
2. You may make balls that are small enough to eat with your hands or huge enough to be used as burgers with wet hands.
3. In a large skillet, heat the oil to medium-high heat. The chicken balls should be fried in batches until they are properly browned on both sides, then serve them.

35.CHICKEN MASSAMAN CURRY

Prep Time15 minutes

Cook Time35 minutes

Total Time50 minutes

Servings10

INGREDIENTS

- 4 ounces Massaman curry paste you will have to get this at your local Asian market
- 3 tablespoons vegetable oil
- 28 ounces unsweetened coconut milk full fat from a can
- 1/2 teaspoon ginger you can use fresh, I just used the powder
- 2 tablespoons chopped cilantro
- 2 tablespoons brown sugar packed

- 2 tablespoons fish sauce
- 1 tablespoon lime juice
- 1 tablespoon Worcestershire sauce
- 1 onion sliced thin
- 1 pound chicken Sliced VERY thin, I used partially thawed chicken from the freezer. It's easy to slice.
- 4 medium potatoes peeled, cubed
- 2 carrots peeled, sliced
- 1 tablespoon peanut butter (creamy or crunchy)
- 1/2 cup peanuts
- sriracha sauce To taste. This is what adds the spiciness.
- red pepper flakes to taste
- jasmine rice cooked

INSTRUCTIONS

1. Heat vegetable oil in an extra large saucepan over medium heat. Stir in curry paste; cook and stir for about 2-3 minutes. This is strong, make sure your windows are open and a fan is blowing.
2. Add 1 can coconut milk and stir until well blended. Add ginger, cilantro, sugar, fish sauce, lime juice, and Worcestershire. Bring to a boil.
3. Add onion and chicken. Reduce to a simmer. When chicken is white and cooked through (about 5 min or so) add another can of coconut milk and bring back to a boil.
4. Add remaining ingredients (except for the rice) and stir until everything is well mixed. Cover and simmer for about 15 minutes or until potatoes are no longer crunchy in the middle. Serve hot over Jasmine rice.

36. THAI CASHEW CHICKEN STIR FRY

Prep: 10 mins

Cook: 8 mins

Servings: 4

INGREDIENTS

- 4 tbsp peanut oil (or canola or vegetable oil)
- 1 cup raw cashews , unsalted (Note 1 for roasted)
- 2 garlic clove , finely minced
- 1 onion (brown, yellow, or white), cut into thin wedges
- 400g/14oz chicken thighs , skinless and boneless, sliced into 1cm / 1/3" thin strips (Note 2)
- 4 green onions , cut into 2.5cm / 1" lengths, white part separated from green part
- 1 red cayenne pepper , deseeded and finely sliced on the diagonal (omit or reduce if preferred) (Note 3)

SAUCE:

- 2 tbsp oyster sauce (Note 4)
- 2 tsp dark soy sauce (Note 5)
- 4 tsp fish sauce (Note 6)
- 2 tsp white sugar
- 6 tbsp water

SERVING:

- Red chilli , finely sliced (optional garnish)
- Jasmine rice , for serving (or other rice of choice)

INSTRUCTIONS

Sauce:

1. Mix all the Sauce ingredients in a small bowl.
2. Cook cashews: Set up a wok or big pan with medium-high heat and add the oil. You may have to eat one to see if it's done.) Cook the cashews for another 5 minutes until they're golden brown and crispy. Remove with a slotted spoon from the skillet.

Garlic and onion:

1. a match made in heaven. Make sure that the temperature is at its highest setting. Add onion and garlic. A minute and a half is all that is needed.

Chicken:

1. Include chicken in your meal. Make sure the exterior turns from pink to white by cooking it for one minute at a time.
2. White part of green onion & chilli: Add the white portion of the green onion and the chilli. Take the chicken out of the oven and let it rest for a minute before serving.

Add Sauce:

1. It should thicken to a syrup in about a minute, and the chicken should be properly coated with it.

Green onion & cashews:

1. Mix in the green portion of the green onions and the cashews. 30 seconds of tossing should enough.

Serve:

1. Serve on a serving platter. Garnish with more red chilli (if you can stand the heat!) and jasmine rice, or any other rice of your preference.

37. PINEAPPLE CHICKEN SATAY

Total: 20 mins

Yield: 4 servings

INGREDIENTS

- ¼ cup lower-sodium soy sauce
- ¼ cup sweet chili sauce (such as Mae Ploy)
- ¼ cup natural-style, crunchy peanut butter
- 2 teaspoons peanut oil
- ½ teaspoon curry powder
- 1 pound chicken breast tenders, cut lengthwise into 8 pieces
- Cooking spray
- 1 ½ cups diced pineapple
- ⅓ cup vertically sliced red onion
- 2 tablespoons chopped fresh cilantro
- 2 tablespoons fresh lime juice
- ⅛ teaspoon ground red pepper

INSTRUCTIONS

1. Whisk together the first three ingredients in a bowl.
2. Toss the chicken, peanut oil, and curry powder together in a bowl. Take eight 6-inch skewers and thread them with chicken.

3. Grilling pan should be heated at medium-high heat. Apply cooking spray to the pan. Chicken should be cooked for 4 minutes on each side or until it is done.
4. Add 2 teaspoons of lime juice, 2 tablespoons of cilantro and 1/8 teaspoon of red pepper to 1 1/2 cups of pineapple while the chicken is cooking. Toss chicken with a combination of soy sauce and pineapple juice, and then serve.

38. THAI GREEN PRAWN CURRY

Prep: 10 mins

Cook: 5 mins

Serves 1

INGREDIENTS

- 1 tbsp sunflower oil
- 1 shallot, finely chopped
- 2 garlic cloves, finely chopped
- 1-2 tbsp Thai green curry paste, or to taste
- 125ml coconut milk
- 75g sugar snap peas, thickly sliced diagonally
- 85g cooked prawns, peeled
- 1 tsp soy sauce
- 1 tsp lemon juice
- small handful coriander, chopped, to serve
- noodles, to serve

INSTRUCTIONS

1. Heat the oil in a wok or big pot. Add the shallot and garlic, and stir-fry for 1-2 minutes. Add the curry paste, coconut cream and 50ml water, and bubble for 2 mins.
2. Add the sugar snap peas and simmer for 1-2 minutes until just beginning to soften. Add the prawns, soy sauce and lemon juice and heat through. Stir in the coriander and serve straight away with noodles.

39. THAI MONKFISH CURRY

Prep: 20 mins

Cook: 20 mins

Total: 40 mins

Yield: 3 servings

INGREDIENTS

- 1 tablespoon peanut oil
- ½ sweet onion, finely chopped
- 1 red bell pepper, chopped
- 3 tablespoons red Thai curry paste
- 1 (14 ounce) can coconut milk
- 12 ounces monkfish, cut into cubes
- 1 tablespoon fish sauce
- 2 tablespoons lime juice
- 2 tablespoons cilantro, chopped

INSTRUCTIONS

1. In a large saucepan, heat peanut oil to medium-high heat. Add chopped onion and simmer for 3 to 5 minutes, until softened and transparent. After 3 to 5 minutes, add the red bell pepper and simmer for another 3 to 5 minutes. Stir in the curry paste and simmer for a further one minute. Then, add the coconut milk and bring it to a boil.
2. Simmer monkfish cubes in coconut milk for 7 to 10 minutes, until the fish is solid and the center is no longer opaque, then remove from heat. Before serving, add fish sauce, lime juice, and cilantro.

40.THAI YELLOW CHICKEN CURRY WITH POTATOES

TOTAL TIME: 40 minutes

YIELD: 6

INGREDIENTS

- 1 tablespoon oil
- half a yellow onion, sliced thinly
- 1 pound boneless skinless chicken breasts, cut into bite-sized pieces
- 1/3 cup yellow curry paste
- 10 baby golden yukon potatoes, cut into bite-sized pieces
- 1 14-ounce can coconut cream (it's like coconut milk, but even more luscious)
- 1/2 – 1 cup water
- 2 teaspoons fish sauce (optional)
- 1–2 tablespoons brown sugar (optional)
- cilantro and rice for serving

INSTRUCTIONS

1. In a big saucepan, heat the oil to medium low heat. Sauté the onions for a few minutes until they're aromatic and softened, then remove from the heat. Add the chicken and curry paste; cook for about 3 to 5 minutes, or until the chicken is cooked through. Curry paste should be mixed in with the potatoes before they're added.
2. Cook the chicken and potatoes for 20-30 minutes, stirring occasionally, until the potatoes are tender and the coconut cream has melted. If necessary, add additional water to get the desired sauce consistency.

3. To really amp it up, add the fish sauce and brown sugar at the very end. Seriously, this is amazing. Serve with rice.

41.PAUL MERCURIO'S PORK AND PUMPKIN RED CURRY RECIPE

Serves: 4

Prep: 15 min

Cooking: 2 hr 30 min

INGREDIENTS

- 3tbsp peanut oil
- 1 red onion, halved and sliced
- 1/2 red pepper, cut into thin strips
- 3tbsp Thai red curry paste
- 700g pork neck, cut into 4-5 cm cubes
- 1tbsp tamarind pulp, soaked in 60ml boiling water
- 270ml coconut cream
- 330ml bottle of Duvel (a Belgian ale)
- 4 kaffir lime leaves
- 500g pumpkin, peeled and cut into 3cm chunks
- 3 potatoes, peeled and cut into 8 pieces each
- 8 baby squash, cut in half
- 2 courgettes, cut into rounds
- 1 handful fresh coriander, chopped sliced red chilli, to serve (optional)

INSTRUCTIONS

1. 180°C/350°F/Gas Mark 4 in the oven.
2. Over medium-high heat, add the oil to a flame-proof casserole dish. Stir-fry the onion and pepper until they are just beginning to brown. Stir in the curry paste and simmer for a few minutes, until it's aromatic and well-combined, then remove from heat.
3. Cook for a few minutes over high heat, stirring constantly, after which you may remove the pork from the pan. Tamarind liquor, coconut cream and beer are all mixed together with a thorough stir. Cook for a few minutes until it's just beginning to thicken. Stir in the veggies and bring the mixture to a boil once more.
4. Remove the pan from the heat, cover it with a lid, and place it in the preheated oven for 30 minutes. Once every half hour, toss in the curry and bake for an additional 1 12 hours.
5. Bake the squash and courgette for a further 45 minutes, or until they are tender to your liking.
6. It's easy to prepare a rich pumpkin sauce by roasting pumpkin until it breaks down entirely.
7. Coriander can be sprinkled on top. Garnish with the remaining coriander and chilli slices if preferred, then serve the curry in large bowls over rice.

42. EASY COCONUT SHRIMP CURRY

PREP: 10 MINS

COOK: 12 MINS

TOTAL: 22 MINS

SERVES: 4

INGREDIENTS

SHRIMP:

- 1 teaspoon garam masala
- 1/2 teaspoon ground cumin
- 1/2 teaspoon turmeric (or curry powder)
- 3/4 teaspoon salt
- 1/4 teaspoon red chili powder
- 1 1/2 tablespoons oil, divided
- 1 pound (500g) peeled Jumbo-sized shrimp, tails on or off

SAUCE:

- 1 tablespoon cooking oil
- 1 tablespoon butter
- 1 onion, finely chopped
- 5 cloves garlic, minced
- 2 teaspoons minced ginger
- 1 1/2 teaspoons garam masala
- 1 1/2 teaspoons ground cumin
- 1 teaspoon ground coriander
- 1 teaspoon turmeric powder or curry powder
- 14 oz. (400g) can crushed tomatoes, or Passata for a smoother sauce

- 1/2-1 teaspoon red chili powder, adjust to your taste preference
- 1 teaspoon salt
- 1 1/2 teaspoons brown sugar
- 13.5 fl oz (400ml) can coconut milk, or coconut cream
- 2 tablespoons freshly chopped cilantro, to garnish

INSTRUCTIONS

SHRIMP:

1. Combine the ingredients in a dish and serve with shrimp. Toss the shrimp in 1 tbsp. oil and the seasonings. Set away for a later time.
2. In a large skillet, heat 1/2 tbsp. oil over medium-high heat. When you're done searing the shrimp, move them to a serving dish. Set away for a later time.

SAUCE:

1. In a large pan or skillet, heat the remaining oil and butter over medium-high heat. Scrape the bottom of the pan with a spatula to remove any browned pieces from the shrimp.
2. Then, add the garlic and ginger and cook for about a minute, or until the garlic and ginger are fragrant. Ground cumin, ground coriander, and turmeric to the garam masala mixture (or curry powder). Cook for about 20 seconds, stirring often, until aromatic.
3. Toss in smashed tomatoes, chili powder, sugar and coconut milk/cream. Allow the mixture to boil for approximately 4 minutes, until it has thickened a bit.
4. Cook for a another minute or two until the shrimp is cooked and heated thoroughly.

5. Remove the heat right away. Make your own naan bread and serve it with fresh garlic butter rice and chopped cilantro for garnish.

43. VEGAN BROCCOLI CHICKPEA CURRY

Total Time: 30 minutes

Yield: 6 servings

INGREDIENTS

- 1 tablespoon coconut oil or avocado oil
- 1 medium white onion, diced
- 3 cloves garlic, minced
- 1 teaspoon freshly minced ginger
- 2 teaspoons curry powder
- 1 teaspoon turmeric
- 1 teaspoon ground ginger
- ½ teaspoon garlic powder
- ¼ teaspoon cayenne powder optional, if you want it spicy
- 1 teaspoon kosher salt, add more to taste
- 2 carrots, sliced into thin coins
- 5 cups broccoli florets
- 1 can chickpeas, drained and rinsed
- 1 (15 ounce) can light coconut milk
- 1¼ cups vegetable broth
- ¼ cup creamy peanut butter
- 2 cups fresh spinach
- Juice of ½ a lime

To serve:

- Rice
- Lime wedges
- Chopped peanuts
- Microgreens

INSTRUCTIONS

1. Using an oven mitt, place a medium-sized pot on the stove over medium heat. Make a frying pan with oil and add the onion to it. Saute for about 5 minutes, or until the onion is transparent. Toss in the spices and heat for a further minute before adding the garlic.
2. Afterward, add in the carrots, broccoli, chickpeas, and coconut milk.
3. Let simmer for 10 minutes or until the broccoli is cooked, then remove the lid.
4. In a medium-sized saucepan, combine the peanut butter, spinach, and water and bring to a boil. Add the lime juice to the curry and mix it in with the rest of the ingredients.
5. With lime wedges, chopped peanuts, and/or microgreens, serve on rice

44. THAI GREEN CURRY

Prep: 15 mins

Cook: 20 mins

Total: 35 mins

Servings4 people

INGREDIENTS

CURRY - USE ONE:

- 4 - 6 tbsp Thai Green Curry Paste (Maesri best) OR (Note 1)
- 1 quantity homemade green curry paste (Note 1)
- EXTRAS - FOR JAR CURRY PASTE (NOTE 2):
- 2 large garlic cloves , minced
- 2 tsp fresh ginger , finely grated
- 1 tbsp lemongrass paste (Note 2)

GREEN CURRY:

- 2 tbsp vegetable oil
- 1 cup (250ml) chicken or vegetable broth, low sodium
- 400 g/14oz coconut milk , full fat (Note 4)
- 1 - 3 tsp fish sauce *
- 1 - 3 tsp white sugar *
- 1/8 tsp salt *
- 6 kaffir lime leaves , torn in half (Note 5)
- 350 g/12 oz chicken thigh , skinless boneless, sliced (Note 6)
- 2 Japanese eggplants, , small, 1cm / 2/5" slices (Note 7)
- 1 1/2 cups snow peas , small, trimmed

- 16 Thai basil leaves (Note 8)
- Juice of 1/2 lime , to taste

GARNISHES:

- Crispy fried Asian shallots , high recommended (Note 9)
- Thai basil or cilantro/coriander , recommended
- Green or red chillies slices , optional
- Steamed jasmine rice

INSTRUCTIONS

1. Medium-high heat is ideal for heating oil in a hefty pan or pot.
2. Take a look at the video to see how long it takes to "dry out" the curry paste (and whether you're using garlic, ginger, and lemongrass Extras). Make sure you don't breathe in the noxious gasses.
3. Dissolve the paste by adding chicken broth and coconut milk to the mixture and mixing thoroughly.
4. Seasonings in a jar: Fish sauce, sugar, and no salt are all that is needed.
5. Seasonings for making your own curry paste:. Remove from heat and stir in 1/8 teaspoon salt and 1/8 teaspoon of fish sauce to taste.
6. Add kaffir lime leaves to the mixture. Bring the mixture to a boil, then lower the heat and simmer for a while.
7. It should be simmering but not scalding at this point, so add the chicken and mix it in. Cook for 7 minutes.
8. Add the eggplants and simmer for another 5 minutes, or until they're soft and mushy.
9. The sauce should be tasted. To increase the saltiness, use fish sauce or salt; to sweeten, use sugar.

10. Stir in the basil and lime juice, and simmer for another 2 minutes until the snow peas are a little mushy. The sauce should still be thin, not thick, after reducing, but that's how it should be. Sauce can deepen if you keep it at a simmer for too long.
11. Curry can be served with jasmine rice and other garnishes, such as saffron.

45.CURRIED COCONUT CHICKEN

Prep: 20 mins

Cook: 50 mins

Total: 1 hr 10 mins

Yield: 6 serving

INGREDIENTS

- 2 pounds boneless skinless chicken breasts, cut into 1/2-inch chunks
- 1 teaspoon salt and pepper, or to taste
- 1 ½ tablespoons vegetable oil
- 2 tablespoons curry powder
- ½ onion, thinly sliced
- 2 cloves garlic, crushed
- 1 (14 ounce) can coconut milk
- 1 (14.5 ounce) can stewed, diced tomatoes
- 1 (8 ounce) can tomato sauce
- 3 tablespoons sugar

INSTRUCTIONS

1. Make a simple seasoning of salt and pepper for the chicken pieces.
2. For two minutes, heat the oil and curry powder in a medium-sized pan over medium-high heat. For a final 1 minute, add the onion and garlic and continue cooking. Toss the chicken in the curry oil and then add it to the pan. At this point, the chicken should no longer be pink in the middle and its fluids should be clear.
3. Toss in the sugar and coconut milk and mix until well-combined. Simmer, covered, for 30 to 40 minutes, stirring regularly.

46.SWEET THAI SHRIMP CURRY WITH PEANUT NOODLES.

Prep Time: 15 MINUTES

Cook Time: 10 MINUTES

Total Time: 25 MINUTES

Servings: 6 Servings

INGREDIENTS

Peanut noodles

- 1 box brown rice noodels 8oz
- 1 cup canned coconut milk
- 1/4 cup creamy peanut butter
- 1 1/2 tablespoons brown sugar

- 1 tablespoon soy sauce
- 3/4 teaspoon red curry paste

Shrimp

- 1/2 cup sweet Thai chili sauce
- 1/3 cup coconut milk
- 1 lime juiced
- 2 tablespoons red curry paste less if you don't like the heat
- 1 tablespoon peanut butter
- 1/2 tablespoon soy sauce
- 1 tablespoon brown sugar
- 1 teaspoon fresh ginger grated
- 2 cloves garlic grated or minced
- 1 red bell pepper sliced
- 1 oz bag sugar snap peas 8
- 1 pound of raw deveined shrimp
- chopped peanut for garnish

INSTRUCTIONS

1. To create the peanut sauce. Mix together 1 cup of canned coconut milk, 2 tablespoons peanut butter, 1 tablespoon of soy sauce, 1 1/2 teaspoons brown sugar, and 3/4 teaspoon of curry paste in a bowl or measuring cup and stir until well combined. Set away for a later time. The water should be at a rolling boil in a big saucepan.
2. Make the shrimp while the water is coming to a boil. Sweet Thai chili sauce, coconut milk, lime juice and red curry paste are all mixed together in a big pan with a sloping rim. Bring the ingredients to a boil, then decrease the heat to a simmer and cook for 3-4 minutes, or until the sauce is somewhat thickened. Whisk everything

together well. After that, add the red pepper and snap peas and simmer for 6 minutes, or until crisp and tender. Shrimp can be added and cooked for 3 minutes. Warm up.

3. Cook the brown rice noodles for 3 to 4 minutes in the boiling water. Place in a wide basin after draining. Toss the noodles with as much of the peanut sauce as you prefer. Shrimp and noodles are ready to be served. If preferred, garnish with chopped peanuts and cilantro!

47.PANANG CURRY

PREP: 15 MINS

COOK 25 MINS

TOTAL: 40 MINS

SERVINGS: 5

INGREDIENTS

- 1 tablespoon oil
- 2 tablespoons Panang curry paste *
- 1 tablespoon peanut butter
- 2 pounds chicken breasts , cut into pieces against the grain
- 1 small onion , sliced
- 1 green bell pepper , thinly sliced
- 1 red bell pepper , thinly sliced
- 2 teaspoons freshly grated ginger
- 4 garlic cloves , minced
- 2 14 oz cans coconut milk (Chaokoh brand is my favorite)
- 2 teaspoons cornstarch
- 1/4 cup light brown sugar , packed

- 1 tablespoons fish sauce
- 1 tablespoon lime juice
- 1 cup loosely packed basil leaves , roughly chopped
- Hot cooked rice white, brown or jasmine

INSTRUCTIONS

1. In a large nonstick skillet, heat the oil to medium-high heat. Add bell peppers, garlic, and ginger to the onions and cook for 2 more minutes.
2. Add the curry paste and peanut butter and cook for a further one minute. Toss in 1 12 cups of coconut milk. Add the cornstarch-coconut milk mixture to the pan and bring to a boil. Stir well.
3. Stir in the chicken until it is well-coated. Cook for 10 to 15 minutes, or until the chicken is no longer pink and the sauce has thickened somewhat.
4. Add sugar, fish sauce, lime juice, and basil to the mixture. For 5 minutes, bring the water to a boil, then reduce the heat and simmer. Add a little of salt and pepper to your liking.
5. Serve with hot, cooked rice.

Chapter 6: Inspiring Thai Veggie Delights

48.STIR-FRIED MUSHROOMS WITH BABY CORN

Prep: 10 mins

Cook: 15 mins

Total: 25 mins

Yield: 4 servings

INGREDIENTS

- 2 tablespoons cooking oil
- 3 cloves garlic, minced
- 1 onion, diced
- 8 baby corn ears, sliced
- ⅔ pound fresh mushrooms, sliced
- 1 tablespoon fish sauce
- 1 tablespoon light soy sauce
- 1 tablespoon oyster sauce
- 2 teaspoons cornstarch
- 3 tablespoons water
- 1 red chile pepper, sliced
- ¼ cup chopped fresh cilantro

INSTRUCTIONS

1. On medium heat, sauté the garlic in the oil for 5 to 7 minutes, until it is browned and fragrant. 5 to 7 minutes after putting in the onion, add the baby corn and cook for another 5 to 7 minutes. Stir in the mushrooms and simmer for approximately 2 minutes, or until they begin to soften. It is important to integrate all of the seasonings into the mixture before serving.

2. A tiny bowl is all that is needed to dissolve the cornstarch and water into the water; add the mixture to the mushrooms. Take care not to overcook the mixture. Garnish with the chile pepper and cilantro before serving in a serving dish.

49.SESAME GINGER BOK CHOY

PREP TIME: 10 minutes

COOK TIME: 6 minutes

TOTAL TIME: 16 minutes

SERVINGS: 4

INGREDIENTS

- 1 tablespoon vegetable oil
- 2 cloves garlic crushed and chopped
- 1 teaspoon fresh ginger
- 8 heads baby bok choy
- 1 teaspoon sesame oil
- 1 tablespoon soy sauce
- 1 tablespoon water
- ¼ teaspoon chili flakes
- sesame seeds for garnish

INSTRUCTIONS

1. In a small bowl, combine sesame oil, soy sauce, water, and red pepper flakes. Set away for a later time.
2. In a large pan, heat the oil over medium heat and sauté the garlic and ginger until they begin to brown, about a minute or two.

3. Add the bok choy whites and cook for an additional 3-4 minutes. Pour in the soy sauce mixture and simmer for another 2 minutes, or until the leaves are wilted and the sauce is cooked through.
4. Serve with sesame seeds as a topping.

50. THE EASIEST VEGETABLE STIR FRY

PREP TIME: 10 MINUTES

COOK TIME: 5 MINUTES

TOTAL TIME: 15 MINUTES

SERVINGS: 6

INGREDIENTS

- 1 tablespoon olive oil
- 1 red bell pepper sliced
- 1 yellow bell pepper sliced
- 1 cup sugar snap peas
- 1 cup carrots sliced
- 1 cup mushrooms sliced
- 2 cups broccoli
- 1 cup baby corn
- 1/2 cup water chestnuts
- ¼ cup soy sauce
- 3 garlic cloves minced
- 3 Tablespoons brown sugar
- 1 teaspoon sesame oil
- 1/2 cup chicken broth
- 1 tablespoon cornstarch
- chopped green onions and sesame seeds for garnish optional

INSTRUCTIONS

1. Add 1 Tablespoon of olive oil to a wok or big pan and heat over medium-high heat. Peppers, carrots, peas and water chestnuts are all good additions. Sauté the vegetables for a few more minutes until they're nearly done.
2. Soy sauce, garlic, brown sugar, sesame oil, chicken broth, and cornstarch are mixed together in a small bowl.
3. Serve with a side of steamed rice or couscous. Sprinkle sesame seeds or chopped green onions on top if desired.

51.THAI MORNING GLORY STIR FRY

DESCRIPTION

- Stir-fried morning glories is one of the simplest Thai foods you'll ever cook, whether as a side dish or a quick lunch. You only need seven ingredients and five minutes to prepare a delicious Thai meal.
- As a side dish, this recipe serves four people. It's plenty for two people to eat for lunch or supper if you serve it with rice.

INGREDIENTS

- 4 cloves garlic
- 4 bird eye chillies – sliced in half lengthways*
- 200g morning glory – rinsed and cut into 2-3 inch pieces
- 1 tbsp fermented soybean paste (also known as yellow bean sauce)*
- 2 tbsp vegetarian oyster or mushroom sauce*
- 1 tsp vegan fish sauce*

- 1 tsp sugar
- ⅛ cup water
- 1 tbsp vegetable oil

INSTRUCTIONS

1. In a pestle and mortar, grind the garlic and chilies to a fine powder.
2. Add the vegetable oil to a wok and bring it to a boil.
3. Simmer for 10 seconds before adding the garlic.
4. Stir in the other ingredients for around 90 seconds.
5. The dish can be served as a side or accompanied by jasmine rice for lunch or supper.

52.AUTHENTIC THAI PUMPKIN STIR FRY RECIPE

Prep Time: 5 mins

Cook Time: 5 mins

Servings: 2

INGREDIENTS

- 1 hand-sized piece pumpkin or squash (see 'ingredient notes' for varieties you can use and a photo showing the size of the piece I used).
- 5 cloves garlic
- 1 tbsp vegetable oil
- About half a large wineglass of water
- Half tsp sugar
- 1 tbsp fish sauce
- 1 tbsp light soy sauce

- 1 egg
- 1 handful (50g) Thai basil – a handful (optional – see note)

INSTRUCTIONS

Preparation:

1. Remove the pumpkin's seeds. There may be some inedible peel on the kind you're using, so you'll want to remove it before cooking. Thinly slice the pumpkin. See the "cooking notes" for more information and a picture.
2. In a pestle and mortar or if you don't have one, mince your garlic in a Thai-style fashion (if you don't have one, simply finely slice the cloves).
3. Set aside the Thai basil leaves if you're using them.
4. Prepare the other ingredients so that they are ready to be added to the wok at any time.

Cooking:

1. Using a wok, add the vegetable oil and heat it up to a high temperature
2. Add the garlic to the oil when it's heated. Cook for a few seconds, then stir-fry for another 10 seconds.
3. Crushed garlic for pad fak tong is fried in oil with five cloves of garlic.
4. Slice the pumpkin and toss with the oil and garlic until well-coated. Stir fry for around 20 seconds.
5. Bring the pumpkin slices up to a half-way point in water (judge this by eye rather than religiously adding half a wineglass). As a general rule, it's better to add too little at this point than too much, as you can always add more if it gets too dry at any time. In addition, add fish sauce, soy sauce, and sugar.

6. A wok filled with water and a half of a pumpkin shows the correct cooking level (half of the pumpkin is submerged). Thai pumpkin stir fry

7. Pumpkin should be tender enough to eat by the time it is done cooking. Alternatively, you may use your cooking spoon to verify whether or not the pumpkin is cooked by poking a little bit of it with it. The size of your wok and the thickness of your pumpkin slices will determine the cooking time. Cooking time for thin slices is likely to be 1-2 minutes. Keep an eye out for dry patches and add water if necessary.

8. To add the egg, you must wait until the pumpkin is almost done. With a spoon, make a well in the center of the pumpkin and add the crackers. With a spoon, softly scramble the yolk.

9. Scrambled egg, freshly cracked into pad fak tong cooking broth, is just becoming opaque.

10. In order to get an opaque yolk, cook the egg for one more minute (20 seconds or so, around about the point in the above picture). After that, use a whisk to incorporate the egg throughout the entire dish.

11. You can add the Thai basil at this stage if you'd like.

12. It just takes a few seconds after the last stir for the egg to be done cooking. Make one last check to ensure the pumpkin is cooked and the spice is accurate before putting it on the table for guests. You may also add a little additional water if necessary.

13. Place on a serving platter and serve immediately.

53.MANGO RICE PUDDING

Prep: 5 min. Cook: 50 min.

4 servings

INGREDIENTS

- 2 cups water
- 1/4 teaspoon salt
- 1 cup uncooked long grain brown rice
- 1 medium ripe mango
- 1 cup vanilla soy milk
- 2 tablespoons sugar
- 1/2 teaspoon ground cinnamon
- 1 teaspoon vanilla extract
- Chopped peeled mango, optional

INSTRUCTIONS

1. Bring water and salt to a boil in a big, heavy pot; add rice. The water should be absorbed and the rice should be soft after 35-40 minutes of simmering.
2. Peel, seed, and slice the mango while you're at it. You may use a potato masher or fork to mash up the mango.
3. Mix rice with milk, sugar, cinnamon, and mashed mango. Cover and cook for another 10-15 minutes, or until the water is mostly absorbed, stirring often.
4. Remove from the heat and toss in the vanilla. If preferred, garnish with diced mango and serve warm or cold.

54. FRESH FRUIT BOWL

Prep: 15 min. + chilling

16 servings

INGREDIENTS

- 8 cups fresh melon cubes
- 1 to 2 tablespoons corn syrup
- 1 pint fresh strawberries, halved
- 2 cups fresh pineapple chunks
- 2 oranges, sectioned
- Fresh mint leaves, optional

DIRECTIONS

1. Combine the melon cubes and corn syrup in a large bowl and mix well. Refrigerate overnight with the lid on. Remaining fruit should be added just before serving. If desired, garnish with fresh mint leaves.

55.GREEN BANANA FRIES

Prep: 10 mins

Cook: 30 mins

Total: 40 mins

Yield: 6 servings

INGREDIENTS

- 5 small unripe (green) bananas
- 1 quart oil for frying, or as needed
- salt to taste

INSTRUCTIONS

1. Because they aren't quite ripe, you'll have to use a knife to remove the skins. Make fries by slicing into long, thin strips or threads.
2. Over medium-high heat, add the oil to a heavy, deep skillet. Make sure the oil is heated to 375 degrees Fahrenheit in your deep-fryer (190 degrees C). Fry the banana fries in the heated oil for 5 to 7 minutes until they are golden brown. Drain on paper towels after removing from the oil. Salt & pepper to taste after removing the excess oil. Serve right away.

56.GREEN PAPAYA SALAD

YIELD: 4 to 6 servings

TIME: 20 minutes

INGREDIENTS

- 1 large or 2 small cloves garlic, peeled
- ¼ teaspoon salt
- 1 tablespoon dry-roasted salted peanuts, more for garnish
- 2 fresh bird chilies or serrano chilies, sliced
- ½ teaspoon raw sugar or white sugar
- 1 tablespoon dried shrimp (optional)
- 2 tablespoons fresh lime juice
- 1 to 2 tablespoons fish sauce (nam pla), to taste
- 2 plum tomatoes, 1 large round tomato, or 8 grape tomatoes, coarsely chopped
- ½ pound long beans, trimmed and cut into 1 1/2-inch lengths (optional)
- 1 small to medium green (unripe) papaya (see Note)
- Lettuce for serving (optional)

INSTRUCTIONS

1. The following ingredients should be mixed or pounded into a paste: garlic powder, salt, peanuts, chiles, sugar, and shrimp (if used). Mix with lime juice and fish sauce in a big bowl when the chicken has been removed from the heat. Add the tomatoes and beans (if using) to a bowl and mix lightly with a spoon (or the mortar).

2. Remove the seeds and membrane from the papaya before grating or shredding the fruit. There should be anything from four to six cups.
3. Toss in the papaya with a gentle hand, but make sure it's well-coated with the dressing. Salt and pepper to taste. Place in a dish (if desired, line bowl with lettuce leaves beforehand). Serve with a sprinkle of peanuts on top.

57. GINGER SOY CHICKEN OVER JASMINE RICE

prep time: 40 MINUTES

cook time: 20 MINUTES

total time: 1 HOUR

INGREDIENTS

- 2 cups Minute Instant Jasmine Rice

Marinade:

- 3 Tablespoons Light Soy Sauce
- 2 cloves garlic, minced
- 1 Tablespoon ginger, grated
- 1/4 cup brown sugar
- 1/2 Tablespoon cooking oil
- pepper

Chicken:

- 8 boneless, skinless chicken thighs
- 1 Tablespoon cooking oil

Garnishes:

- 2 green onions, sliced
- 2 teaspoons sesame seeds

INSTRUCTIONS

1. Cook the Minute Instant Jasmine Rice according to the instructions on the package.
2. Pour marinade ingredients into a small basin and mix thoroughly.
3. In a Ziploc bag or small dish, marinate the chicken thighs.
4. Put it in the fridge for at least a half hour and up to a day to chill.
5. A big skillet should be preheated to medium-high heat after marinating the chicken. Toss in a tablespoon of frying oil.
6. Swirl the pan in the oil to coat it.
7. 4 pieces of chicken should be added and fried until they are golden on both sides and cooked through.
8. Make sure to serve the chicken on a clean dish. The following four pieces should be cooked in a pan.
9. Pour the marinade into the skillet and bring it to a boil when the chicken is done cooking. Keep whisking until the marinade thickens into a glaze.
10. Put the chicken back in the skillet and turn off the heat.
11. Dredge the chicken in the heavy sauce with a spoon.
12. Sprinkle sesame seeds and scallions on top.
13. Place on top of the rice.
14. Serve right away.

58. THAI RICE PUDDING

Prep: 10 mins

Cook: 15 mins

Total: 25 mins

Servings: 3 to 4 servings

INGREDIENTS

- 2 cups Thai sweet rice
- 3 1/2 cups water
- 1/2 teaspoon salt
- 1/2 cup canned coconut milk
- 3/4 cup sugar, any kind, to taste
- 1 teaspoon pure vanilla extract
- 1 teaspoon ground cinnamon
- 1/4 teaspoon ground nutmeg
- 1/4 teaspoon ground cloves
- 1 pod star anise, for optional garnish
- 1 cinnamon stick, for optional garnish
- 3 tablespoons crushed peanuts, for optional garnish
- 1 cup toasted coconut, for optional garnish

INSTRUCTIONS

1. Gather the ingredients.
2. Add 2 cups of water to a big saucepan and cook the rice. Allow 10 to 30 minutes of soaking time.
3. Salt and the remaining 1 1/2 cups of water should be added once this time has elapsed. Stir well.
4. Take a saucepan and put it on the stove. Immediately after it reaches a boil, lower the heat to medium-low and

cover the pot with a lid that is slightly awry, allowing some steam to vent.

5. To cook the rice, bring water to a boil and let it simmer for about 15 to 20 minutes, or until all of the water is absorbed.

6. But don't turn off the heat completely. For 5 to 10 minutes, keep the rice "steaming" with the cover tightly on.

7. Then, remove the cover and whisk in the coconut milk. You may need to use a spoon or fork to break up the rice a bit since the lower temperature causes it to cling together.

8. Add 3/4 cup to 1 cup of sugar while the mixture is simmering on low heat. You can start with a smaller amount and increase more as necessary.

9. Add the vanilla, cinnamon, nutmeg, and cloves to the mixture.

10. Try the pudding to see whether it's sweet enough. Adding extra sugar or more coconut milk will make the pudding more palatable. In the end, the rice will have absorbed the majority of the coconut milk, resulting in a very thick pudding.

11. Alternatively, you may serve the thick pudding in individual serving dishes and top it with coconut milk, cream, or the milk of your choice, making it easier to spoon into serving containers.

12. Adding a little additional cinnamon or nutmeg to the top of each dish makes a nice finishing touch. Cinnamon sticks, entire star anise, peanut pieces, or toasted coconut can be added to the dish if you choose.

13. Enjoy.

59. THAI MANGO STICKY RICE DESSERT

Prep: 10 mins

Cook: 25 mins

Soak Time: 20 mins

Total: 55 mins

Yield: 3 cups

INGREDIENTS

- 1 cup Thai sweet rice (aka sticky rice)
- 1 1/2 cups water, divided
- 1 (13.5-ounce) can coconut milk, divided
- 1/4 teaspoon salt
- 4 to 5 tablespoons brown sugar, to taste, divided
- 1 to 2 ripe mangoes

INSTRUCTIONS

1. Gather the ingredients.
2. Ingredients for a Thai mango sticky rice dessert
3. Soak the rice in 1 cup of water for 20 to 30 minutes in a medium-sized saucepan. Don't drain the rice!
4. Pouring one cup of water into a pot and soaking Thai sweet rice for an hour
5. Add another half cup of water, along with the salt, the brown sugar, and the rest of the coconut milk. Stir well. Boil the mixture for a few minutes, then slightly cover it (leaving some room for steam to escape). Simmer the mixture over medium-low heat, or until it reaches a low boil.
6. Several tablespoons of brown sugar, salt, and coconut milk are added to the pot.

7. Simmer for around 20 to 30 minutes, or until the rice has absorbed the coconut water. Leave the saucepan on the stove with the lid on firmly, but turn off the heat. Take a few moments to let it to cool down a bit.
8. The sticky rice was cooked in a pot.
9. In a small saucepan, bring the remaining coconut milk to a simmer over medium-low heat (about 5 minutes). To dissolve the brown sugar, use 3 teaspoons. Sauce should be tasted for sweetness, and additional sugar can be added if necessary. Adding it to the rice reduces the sweetness somewhat.
10. In a saucepan, combine the coconut milk and sugar.
11. Slice the mangoes into bite-sized chunks by cutting them open and slicing each one.
12. On a chopping board, mangoes are sliced with a sharp knife.
13. In each serving bowl, add some heated rice and a generous amount of sweet coconut sauce. To resemble an English pudding with custard sauce, the rice should be covered in sauce. A sprinkle of additional sauce and mango slices are the perfect finishing touches to the rice.

60. EASY CREAMY COCONUT BLACK BEANS

PREP: 5mins

COOK: 2hr

TOTAL: 2hr 5mins

INGREDIENTS

- 2 cups dried black beans, picked through, rinsed (about 1 pound), *not currently tested with canned beans
- 3 cloves garlic, smashed and peeled
- 1/2 medium onion, peeled, left unchopped
- 1 bay leaf
- 1 teaspoon ground cumin
- 1/8 teaspoon ground cinnamon
- 1 3/4 cups can unsweetened coconut milk, see notes
- Water
- Salt and ground black pepper
- Handful fresh cilantro
- 1 lime
- Optional toppings: Tomatoes, avocado and cheese

INSTRUCTIONS

1. A big saucepan should be filled with all of the ingredients, including the coconut milk and all of the other mentioned spices. 2 inches of water should be used to cover the beans. Put over high heat, then lower to a moderate simmer after bringing to a rolling boil. After 1 1/2 to 2 hours, remove the lid and continue cooking the beans until they are soft. Stir the beans occasionally while cooking, and add more water if necessary if they appear to be drying out.

2. Remove the onion, garlic, and bay leaf when the beans are done cooking. Toss in a pinch of salt and some freshly ground black pepper, and taste again. Turn the heat up to medium-high and quickly simmer the mixture. Cook the beans for 5 to 10 minutes, stirring often, until the liquid thickens. Serve with lime wedges and chopped fresh cilantro. Topping the beans with chopped tomatoes and avocado is a delicious addition.

62.TOM YUM FRIED RICE

Prep Time: 30 minutes

Cook Time: 15 minutes

Total Time: 45 minutes

Servings: 6

INGREDIENTS

For The Toppings

- 1 1/4 US cup day old rice (cooked the day before and left in the fridge overnight)
- 70 g / 0.15 lb Chinese broccoli (thinly sliced)
- 90 g / 0.2 lb prawns/shrimp (deveined and peeled)
- 3 tomatoes (finely chopped and seeds removed)
- 2 g / 0.004 lb kaffir lime leaves
- 1 onion (finely chopped)
- 2 red shallot (thinly sliced)
- 2 sprig spring onions (chopped)
- cooking oil

For The Seasoning

- 4 tbsp tom yum paste (or to taste)
- 1 tbsp sugar (or to taste)
- 1/2 tbsp chicken bouillon powder (optional)

INSTRUCTIONS

1. Add three tablespoons of oil to a hot wok and bring to a high heat. Pour in the prawns and simmer for two minutes, or until they're just cooked through.
2. On medium heat, add 3 tbsp oil to the same wok and brown the onion and red shallots for 3 minutes.
3. Add the Chinese broccoli and cook for 2 minutes on high heat, then add the rice. To loosen the grains, keep them moving around in the pan with a continual stirring motion.
4. Add a little amount of tom yum paste to the rice and mix it thoroughly, making sure that all of the grains are covered. Sugar and chicken bouillon powder should be added to the mix.
5. Allowing the grains to cook for a further 2 minutes can help to reduce the amount of water they retain.
6. Toss in the kaffir lime leaves and tomatoes, and then mix thoroughly until they're evenly distributed.
7. Make sure to thoroughly stir in the prawns.
8. Add the spring onions to the rice and toss rapidly until they are evenly distributed.
9. Serve right away with cucumber slices and a sunny side up egg on top!

63. THAI GREEN CURRY FRIED RICE

PREP TIME: 10 mins

COOK TIME: 15 mins

TOTAL TIME: 25 mins

SERVINGS: 4 people

INGREDIENTS

- 3 cloves garlic minced
- 1 tablespoon green curry paste
- 1 medium carrot chopped
- ½ cup green peas (frozen or canned)
- 2 cups cooked cooled rice (see notes)
- ¼ cup coconut milk
- 1 tablespoon soy sauce or tamari

INSTRUCTIONS

1. Cast-iron or nonstick pan with a spoonful of oil over medium heat. The oil can be omitted and replaced with 14 cup of broth or water.
2. Toss in the curry paste and garlic cloves at this point. For 2-3 minutes, heat the oil in a pan.
3. Next, add the carrots and simmer for about 3-4 minutes, until they are softened.
4. Continue to simmer for another 4 to 5 minutes or until the rice is cooked through and the green peas are heated through. Turn the temperature down.
5. Add half of the soy sauce and taste to see if you need more. You may also increase the spiciness by using extra green curry paste.
6. Preferably when it's hot!

64. THAI PINEAPPLE FRIED RICE

Time: 15 minutes

Cook Time: 5 minutes

Total Time: 20 minutes

Servings: 4 servings

INGREDIENTS

- 2 tablespoons vegetable oil
- 2 shallots or 1 small onion, thinly sliced
- 3 cloves garlic, minced
- 1 small red or green chili, minced (de-seeded for milder rice)
- 12 fresh extra-large or jumbo shrimp, peeled and deveined (about 8 ounces depending on their size)
- 2 eggs, beaten
- 3 tablespoons chicken broth or stock
- 3 tablespoons fish sauce
- 2 teaspoons curry powder
- 1 teaspoon sugar
- ½ cup roasted unsalted cashews
- 4 cups cooked rice (preferably at least 1 day old)
- 1 cup pineapple chunks (fresh is better, but canned works too–about half a 20-ounce can)
- ½ cup frozen peas, thawed
- ¼ cup raisins or currants
- 2 scallions, finely sliced

INSTRUCTIONS

1. Over medium-high heat, add oil to a wok or a large nonstick frying pan. One minute later, add the shallots,

garlic, and chili, and stir-fry until fragrant. Add the shrimp and stir them around a few times. If the wok becomes too dry, a small amount of broth or water can be added to moisten it.

2. Set the mixture aside so that the eggs may be added. As though you were cooking scrambled eggs, add the beaten eggs to the pan and cook them rapidly. Combine the shrimp and shallots with the scrambled eggs.
3. A small bowl should be used to mix together the chicken broth, fish sauce, curry powder, sugar, and salt.
4. Stir-fry the cashews for 30 seconds once they've been added.
5. Afterwards, add the rice to the pan, breaking it up if necessary. To get a consistent hue, stir-fry until all rice has been incorporated into the sauce. Take care not to overcook your rice by stirring it constantly; instead, scoop from the bottom of the pan and toss like a salad instead.
6. Add the pineapple, peas, and raisins to the mixture and mix. Taste for seasoning before serving. A further 1 to 2 minutes of stir-frying should be added to the process. Toss in half of the scallions.
7. Sprinkle the leftover scallion on top of the finished dish. The Thais serve it in a pineapple or on a plate.

65.RESTAURANT STYLE COCONUT RICE (COCONUT MILK)

Prep: 2 mins

Cook: 15 mins

Total: 17 mins

Servings4

INGREDIENTS

COCONUT RICE

- 2 cups (360g) jasmin or long grain white rice (Note 1)
- 400 ml / 14 oz coconut milk , full fat or light (Note 2)
- 1/2 cup (125ml) water
- 1 tbsp white sugar (Note 3)
- 1/2 tsp salt
- ASIAN RESTAURANT STYLE - USE ONE:
- 3 pandan leaves , knotted
- 3 kaffir lime leaves , crushed in hand

OPTIONAL GARNISH:

- 1 tbsp desiccated coconut , toasted, to garnish

INSTRUCTIONS

1. Make sure the water is clean by rinsing the rice in it. After draining the rice, soak it in water for 15 minutes. Then, flush.
2. A small pot or big saucepan should be filled with rice, coconut milk, water, sugar, and salt. Consider using pandan or kaffir lime leaf for a more authentic Asian restaurant flavor.

3. Bring it to a boil, then lower the heat to a simmer and stir it once.
4. For the next 14 minutes, you can take a break.
5. Remove from the heat and allow it cool for 10 minutes before serving.
6. Using a rubber spatula, fluffing If desired, top with toasted coconut before serving.

THE END

Printed in Great Britain
by Amazon

73410337R00061